I0411149

TAKING DOWN AMERICA
The Destructive Policies of Barack Obama,
and Hillary Clinton

T.C. Brennan

You shall know the truth…

And the truth shall make you free.

John 8:32

Author's Note:

My family and friends often tell me that I should have been a history professor because of my detailed knowledge of that subject. I will not fault them for that opinion even though they are far from understanding why I do what I do.

They see my knowledge of history as the central interest of my life. Because of this they completely miss the real theme of my life: which is the TRUTH. This is why I have always been interested in history. Because, therein, are great truths: and therefore, great lessons.

And, that's also why I've always been interested in the universe, religions, mysteries and subjects of all sorts. I want to know the truth. It is ONLY from truth that anything of value is learned.

But, to spend your time and your future telling the truth, is a hard, risky and often self-sacrificial thing. There are those that don't want the truth to be told. *I mean that they REALLY don't want the truth to be told...*

Socrates learned this. When confronted with conforming (and not telling the truth) or being executed by THE STATE he chose to drink hemlock and take his own life; therefore ensuring his fate. But, more importantly: by that act, Socrates took away the power of the state. That... is what this book is about.

From Socrates and many, many other great men and women I have learned about in history; I have also learned that to speak the truth you must possess the courage to endure the hostility and attacks of those who oppose it. Those people are generally individuals of dubious character who will tell any lie and use any means at their disposal to silence the truth because not to do so will uncover their nefarious motives, or worse yet: their nefarious deeds, which are most often motivated by their selfish lust for riches and power.

Sometimes though, it's just about their egotistical need *to be right*, thereby validating what they see as *their* superior intelligence. It makes no difference which of the two it is: these people will oppose you equally as vehemently.

Should any of the aforementioned people read this book they will most assuredly have a fits denying all the truths that fill these pages.

TABLE OF CONTENTS

Foreword   9

Appeal to the Next American President   13

ONE.   What Has Obama *Really* Done and What Else Will He Do?   15

TWO.   Domestic Security, Tranquility & Race Relations   31

THREE. Open Borders, Lawlessness and Public Safety   41

FOUR.   Foreign Policy, The War On Terror, National Security   45

FIVE.   Scandals, Corruption and Treachery   57

SIX.   The Two Economies   63

SEVEN. The Vast Left-Wing Conspiracy   67

EIGHT. Barack Obama's REAL Legacy   71

NINE.   The Democratic Party Going Forward   75

TEN.   Hillary's Real History   85

THE CONSTITUTION of the United States of America   99

FOREWORD

I did not want to write this book. After all, Barack Obama only has four months left in office, doesn't he? Well, that's true, but he can do a lot of damage in four months. Pick a subject: the war on terror, national security, the economy, crime, race relations, immigration; you name it. He has just gone from one thing to the next, stifling the economy, raising taxes, causing division, disrupting our society, pitting people against one another, inciting racial unrest and violence; all to the detriment of America.

It didn't take him long to cause damage in any of these areas. Indeed, he has been quite proficient. After considering all of the things that Barack Obama has purposely done to inflict harm on this country, and the fact that he has pursued these anti-American policies even more aggressively once the 2014 Congressional elections were behind him, there is therefore, good reason to believe that this president will be more dangerous to our country in his last few months in office than he has ever been.

Most of the damage Barack Obama has done has never been publicized; or at least it not been attributed to him or his statements, policies, regulations and his prejudices. No honest examination of his motives has ever occurred. Indeed, quite the opposite is true.

President Obama has been protected by the biased American media; from the criticism he richly deserves, and the responsibility he has for the damage he has caused to this country. And now he is going to extraordinary lengths to compromise the security of the country: YOUR country, YOUR security and that of YOUR family. So yes, he can still do a lot of damage.

Obama has been ruling by executive fiat (using executive orders, executive memos and federal agency directives) and bypassing Congress for some time now and this will likely be his method of operation until he is out of the White House. And, unfortunately for all of us, with such a liberal and biased press and media we can't rely on them to honestly or truthfully report on the actions of this president or, for that matter, the left leaning Democratic Party. In short: the media is on his side and the majority of the people comprising American media are *partisan* Democrats who always have, and continue to; cover for their party and in particular for this president, and indeed, have also omitted any negative reporting of the same.

So what are we to do? Well, we can start by telling the truth and taking an honest look at the policies of Barack Obama, and try to conclude from them, what his real motives are and have been from the beginning. That's partly what this book is about and why I wrote it. This book chronicles just some of the catastrophic damage this president and his new Democratic Party have done to this country over the last seven years: not to mention the last fifty years plus of Democratic Party shenanigans.

You might want to look that word up if you're not familiar with it – it's meaning is a lot more sinister than it sounds.

So, why this need to tell the truth now? The answer is simple and… it is CRITICAL. Barack Obama is intent on pushing the limits of his agenda before he leaves office. And his reckless agenda poses extraordinarily severe threats to the security and safety of all Americans.

Ignoring warnings from the directors of both the FBI and The Department of Homeland Security, Barack Obama is bringing as many Syrian refugees here as he can before his term ends. He has been advised by the top officials of all of the government's security agencies that these refugees cannot be vetted for ties to terrorism because there is no way to check their backgrounds. He has been further advised that ISIS members will easily be able to infiltrate this refugee population and that terrorists will more than likely be among these immigrants coming into our country. Still, he refuses to back off of his plan. Instead, he's rushing the poor and inadequate vetting that can be done. *Why?*

It is completely irrational and reckless to bring tens of thousands of Muslim immigrants here without the ability to check their backgrounds. Irrational that is, unless this is part of an agenda. An agenda we know nothing about. An agenda being put into place that does not have the interests of America or its people at heart. *So, just what is his reason for doing this?*

Keep in mind that for over seven years Obama has refused to call Islamic terrorist attacks as Islamic. He has done everything in his power to deflect any criticism of Islam or association of Islam to terrorism; even to the point of branding obvious Islamic terrorist attacks with ridiculous names: i.e., man caused tragedies, etc. He should be so rigid in his defense of The United States, but he's not.

A president's most important responsibility is to protect America's citizens and Obama's policies fly in the face of his oath as president to do this.

Finally, I have written this book because we are about to elect the next president of this country. And this president will have to undo as much of President Obama's destructive policies, laws and regulations as possible in order to mend this once great country before it completely disintegrates.

Yes, I call them destructive policies: because that's what they are. They are **purposely destructive** *and anti-American. And yes, I did say disintegrates because this president and the Democratic Party have done so much damage and caused so much division that this country is indeed, disintegrating right before our eyes.*

The reader should know that Hillary Clinton has said that she fully intends to increase the number of Syrian refugees brought here by more than 5 times! Will they then be vetted any better? The answer is no. She has no way to vet these refugees for terrorist affiliations or to discover if they are radicalized. So then, why would anyone increase the number of these people when they cannot be checked and pose such high risks? *Ask yourself...*

Before you cast your vote for our country's next president I urge you to ask yourself if your candidate will seriously address the damage done by Barack Obama that is chronicled in these pages. Hillary, most certainly, will not.

Hillary Clinton is on record stating that she will not only continue Barack Obama's disastrous and dangerous policies, but that she intends to expand them. Hillary's policies on the major issues are outlined in this book. I urge you to review them.

You might be shocked.... If you're not: you should be.

I also urge all of you to pass on the appeal that I have written on the pages that follow. It is an Appeal to the Next American President (whether that be a man or a woman: whether Republican or Democrat).

T.C. Brennan

****

An Appeal to the Next "American" President

If you are elected to be the next President of the United States then, we the people, wish make to make an appeal... to you.

We the people of the United States of America appeal to you to truly be: an "American" President.

One, who not only believes in our Constitution, but enforces it, preserves it, and defends it: As your oath of office will call you to do.

One who, like Washington, imposes his virtue on the office, and imbues it with dignity.

One who, like Washington, doesn't forego integrity for the sake of approval, or the doctrines of a party.

One who, like Lincoln, has the courage to do what is right... No Matter What The Cost.

We the people of America appeal to you to be a president who sees us as a whole; and not as classes or races; but as a whole people, for whom our Constitution was written. And we ask you to see each of us individually as the object of that Constitution: because as individual Americans; each of is.

We the people, ask you to hold sacred, the trust we place in you for the governance of our country, and the protection of it.

And, we the people, ask you to hold America sacred: because it is.

America can no longer afford political officials who use the powers entrusted in them to their own ends; or those of a party; or those of a class; or those of a race; or those of any other than the whole of us.

America can no longer afford officials in authority, elected or otherwise, who do their will, and not that of the people.

And...America can no longer afford a president who allows any of these to happen: even if tacitly.

If you are now elected to be the next President of the United States, you will then need to be... a president of the people, by the people, and for the people.

You will need to be so because... America needs you to be so.

T.C. Brennan: on behalf of the American people.

****

ONE

What Has Obama *Really* Done and... What Else Will He Do?

In my Foreword I mentioned that Barack Obama is determined to bring tens of thousands of Syrian refugees (he has said 10,000 by September of 2016) into our country in spite of the fact that both the Director of the FBI and the Director of the Department of Homeland Security have said publicly that these people could not be vetted and that **ISIS will infiltrate** the ranks of these refugees thereby allowing many potential terrorists into our country. **This will happen.** It already has in Europe, which is in chaos from these migrants. And you will get to pay for the expenses of these people including their rents, food, healthcare, cell phones and a cash monthly income.

The income given to political refugees is significantly higher than that given to our own citizens for welfare assistance.

Obama's plan to bring in thousands of high-risk refugees is simply insanity and cannot be rationally justified or explained. It can't be explained that is, unless one looks at the history of Obama since he's been in office. Consider that the very first thing Barack Obama did overseas was to apologize to the world for America and, in particular, to the Muslim leaders in the Mid-East in Cairo. This was his infamous "Apology Tour" wherein he blamed the lack of opportunity in Muslim countries and the poverty of Muslims in general on "colonialism." In other words: the exploitation of Muslim countries by white European countries and, of course, America.

That's right: that's what he said. Videos of that Cairo address in 2009 are still online.

Consider the fact that virtually every survey taken here, in Europe, the U.K. and even those throughout the mid-east since 2001 reflect that, minimally, ten percent of all Muslims have radical leanings: and most surveys reflect numbers closer to forty percent. In those same surveys fifty percent of the Muslims surveyed approve of suicide attacks and bombings against western targets and people. Given these facts, bringing thousands of Muslims from that region of the world to the U.S. without the ability to do thorough background checks is lunacy, unless that is: it is part of another agenda.

Consider that Obama would not call obvious terrorist attacks as Islamic or even as acts of terrorism: even when the perpetrators were shouting Allahu Akbar as they slaughtered innocent Americans. For example: it was just last year that Obama allowed his administration to call the barbaric Fort Hood massacre an act of terrorism. For over six years he has insisted that it was workplace violence. This, by the way, caused great difficulties for the servicemen and women who were the victims of that horrible attack and deprived them of benefits that they fully deserved and desperately needed.

Consider also that Barrack Obama has ordered members of The United States military NOT to refer to our terrorist enemies as Islamic terrorists or their actions as those of Islamic extremists, regardless of overwhelming facts that clearly demonstrate that they are indeed Islamic.

And consider this: it was recently reported by whistleblowers that worked in The Department of Homeland Security that in 2009, after just taking office, Barack Obama ordered that the Department of Homeland Security scrub (delete) all of the names of Muslims with ties to the Muslim Brotherhood and Jihadists from its files. Delete: as in permanently erase. *Why?*

Many Americans think that Obama does these things because he is being politically correct. Others think that he does not want to incite more violence on the part of the radical Jihadists and still others think that he is weak and afraid to act more aggressively towards the Islamic radicals. None of these assumptions are correct.

Barack Obama himself is quoted as saying that the most beautiful sound in the world is the Muslim call to prayer. There's nothing wrong with this of course, it reflects his affinity for Islam. There would be nothing wrong with that either if it weren't for his actions and his policies, which have cost so much American blood and treasure overseas, loss of innocent civilian lives within our borders, allowed the spread of ISIS everywhere and are now putting Americans at more risk than they have ever been.

Obama's latest plan to bring many thousands of Muslim refugees to resettle here without any ability to thoroughly vet these individuals presents a "Clear and Present Danger" to The United States of America on an unparalleled level. When Barack Obama announced his intention to bring these refugees here he told us that it would take 18 months to two years for the refugees to go through the vetting process. Yet, his security officials say these refugees can't be vetted properly even in that amount of time. In any case, President Obama's statement was just another lie because now his Administration smugly tells us the process of vetting the refugees will take a mere three months and that there is a huge PUSH to rush even this process up. A deliberate rush to get them here: *Once again: why…?*

This action is so flagrantly dangerous and irresponsible that, (if he were a Republican president), it would most assuredly be grounds for impeachment and his removal from office. Of all of the terrible things that this president has done: this ranks among his worst.

Just think about how hard it is to prevent one terrorist act. Then multiply that by a thousand, or thousands, more. Add to that the fact that the Obama Administration has issued over 600,000 green cards to Muslims over the past five years and that Obama's Administration often waives personal interviews required by the government for people entering the United States *if they are Muslims*: but, not for others; not for Christians for example. On top of that over 500,000 people have over stayed their Visas (many from the Middle East) and Obama's Administration has no idea where they are.

Take the case of Tashfeen Malik. She was one of the two shooters who ruthlessly murdered innocent people in the San Bernardino massacre on December 2, 2015. This woman was never interviewed or checked at all. The interview and background check of her had been waived. Only after the massacre, did we learn that the Obama Administration had waived any examination of this woman and that this laxity with regard to ANY vetting was commonplace with many other Muslims as well. And then, after the attack, Obama took days before he would even call the San Bernardino massacre a terrorist attack: much less a terrorist attack committed by Muslims who had been radicalized.

Why the reticence, Mr. President?

Had Administration officials not waived examination of this woman they would have found her Jihadist rants on facebook and other social media sites, which would have prevented her from entering the country and saved the lives of the many victims in that attack. It was ONLY after this attack that we all learned the shocking truth that preferential treatment was being given to Muslims by the Obama Administration. But you would have not seen this reported on the three major TV networks. If it had been reported at all it would have been a slight comment made to seem trivial. Thankfully, Fox News did catch it and did report it.

This bias for Islam has been evident since Obama first took office and gave his oath to the American people, which he has repeatedly broken; and in the gravest sense.

Early in the year the Whitehouse put out a video of the French president giving an address about the horrific attacks in France and that country's efforts to combat terrorism. But, the Obama Administration DELETED all of his references to Islamic terrorists. *Why?*

I can only hope that those reading this book are beginning to get the picture.

All of the preceding points have to do with recent incidents. In my book, The Un-American President: Barack Obama, I cited many instances of Obama's prejudicial policies and actions that were clearly anti-American and showed favoritism towards Islam during his first term in office.

Since then, if anything: he has gotten bolder. As I said then, any president who was a Republican, having done the things that Barack Obama has done, would have been impeached by now. But with our biased press and media and our spineless Republican Congress, we the people have been given no hope and no defense. No defense at all from this rogue, very much anti-American president.

The Republican establishment is afraid of being branded as racist by the media (and they most certainly would be). The media has repeatedly done this to critics of Obama. On top of that this media omits reporting the truth about Barack Obama, cover for him and deliberately don't report on his terrible decisions or the risks he is imposing on this country.

Barack Obama seems to have disdain and even an animus towards America. White Americans, and in particular, those who are Christian and the religion of Christianity itself, seem to be the objects of this disdain. This is evidenced by his own statements. His infamous "Clinging to their guns and Bibles" statement is just one example of his real attitude towards white, Christian Americans: This derisive comment was made by him in reference to the white, Bible believing Americans that populate the country between the coasts.

Had any white politician made this comment about black Bible believing Americans it would have been very correctly regarded as racist: just as Obama statement should also be understood as a racist remark directed at white Americans. No one will call him on it, though.

Barrack Obama seems to see everything in America through a black vs. white racial prism. Hence his unwarranted interventions and prejudicial actions after the completely justifiable shooting of Michael Brown in Ferguson, Missouri as well as numerous other incidents that he needlessly turned into racial incidents; thereby fomenting racial strife and violence.

Obama's recent address wherein he promoted his plan to bring the Syrian refugees to our country and stumbled through his dissertation on angels and the Christian tradition of looking out for one's neighbors was nauseatingly patronizing, insulting and intended to "guilt" Christian Americans into going along with his dangerous plan. But it only served to show how little Barack Obama knows of the faith and religion of Christianity. It was obvious from his statements that this man knows next to nothing about Christianity. And that church he went to in Chicago... just Google Reverend Jeremiah Wright in Chicago. Watch some of his videos... No one can call that a church.

Doctor Robert Jeffress (a prominent Christian minister) recently gave a nationally televised sermon wherein he recited many of the numerous derogatory statements that Barack Obama has made which denigrate the Bible, its messages and question its wisdom.

With regard to the migrants from the mid-east: it's not like Obama hasn't had a model for what will happen here if he brings in those Syrian refugees. Just look at Europe. It's in chaos. Mobs of Muslim men run wild, sexually assaulting women and committing crimes. Whole sections of cities are under Muslim rule and following Sharia law: untouchable by the authorities of the countries they're in. And, of course, there have been the Paris, Brussels and Nice terrorist attacks: with more to come.

It's so bad in Germany now that they've had to set up separate trains for women to get back and forth to work because of the risk to them from Muslim refugee mobs of men sexually assaulting them. Over 1200 women have been sexually assaulted and raped by these so-called refugees in just this past year and there have been no consequences for these animals.

Finally, the EU (European Union) has reported that ISIS and other Islamic terrorists have **definitely infiltrated** Europe by posing as refugees. They are now on the loose in a borderless Europe.

Of course Obama knows about all of this, but does he care? Obviously, the answer to that question is NO; he doesn't care. He is determined to bring those high-risk refugees here and locate them in communities all over this country. Worse yet, Homeland Security will NOT be allowed to know their whereabouts once here. This is another one of Obama's policies.

Yes, you did read that right... So ask yourself: is this policy simply idiotic; or is it designed to do something else?

There have been many who have suggested to Mr. Obama that "safe zones" be set up in the Middle-East for the Syrian refugees: Those safe territories could be protected by NATO and/or international troops and the cost to the taxpayers of the rescuing countries (such as ours) would be far less. **And... the risk posed by introducing a host of new terrorists into the U.S. domestically would be completely eliminated!** Barack Obama has dismissed this option out of hand without any rational reason for doing so.

Ask yourself why he is so insistent upon bringing the refugees here even when there are cheaper, more expedient and much safer alternatives. AND... alternatives that the refugees themselves prefer!

Yes, ask yourself...

The answer has nothing to do with what is practical or safe; it doesn't even have to do with what the refugees themselves would prefer. It all has to do with his agenda and his continual favoritism of Muslims over the American people, whom Barack Obama took a solemn oath to protect. He is blatantly violating his Presidential Oath by bringing dangerous, potential terrorists into this country in defiance of all of his own security advisors' advice.

This isn't just malfeasance: this jeopardizes our nation's security, gives aid and comfort to our enemies and, if we were in a declared war sanctioned by Congress, would be treasonous. But, don't worry... no one will stand up to him and the biased press will cover for him.

People in Obama's Administration and the Democratic Party pundits are quick to say that he (Obama) has kept us safe.

Oh, really... if Obama's Administration hadn't imposed such heavy handed "political correctness" on our military, Major Nidal Malik Hasan wouldn't have had a chance to gun down and maim so many innocent people at Fort Hood, Texas; much less be promoted to the rank of Major in spite of bells and whistles going off all over the place that he was indeed, a radicalized Muslim. These warnings were blatantly obvious. But no one would come forward for fear of being labeled as a racist or an "Islamophobe." To be either would mean severe ramifications for the person bringing up the issue.

Then there were the Boston Marathon bombings, the San Bernardino massacre and, most recently, the ghastly slaughter at the Pulse nightclub in Orlando. In both the Boston and Orlando cases the FBI had identified the subjects that would later perpetrate these acts of terrorism, but due to the time limits imposed on surveillance by the Obama Administration those individuals were then left to roam freely without further scrutiny.

Then, after the Orlando attack Obama even had the gall to parade Attorney General Loretta Lynch out on the Sunday political talk show circuit to try and *cover up* the fact that the Orlando attack was an attack committed by an Islamic radical. Obama's spokespeople threw out all kinds of alternative explanations for the motives for this attack even though the terrorist had called 911 and declared that he was carrying out the attack for Islam and survivors of the attack heard him say Allahu Akbar during the slaughter.

Then... unbelievably, the Administration took the word Allah out of the transcripts of terrorist's statements made during the attacks: and substituted it with the word God. Why in the world would Obama's Attorney General do that? This juvenile, sophomoric and blatantly untruthful measure was very obviously designed to switch the blame from Islam to something else.

Was this done to shift the blame towards Christian Americans who do use the word God for their deity?

The extent to which Barack Obama will go to deflect negative aspersions of Islam borders on being pathological. He changes facts (even after they are widely known); he tries to shift blame and, in all too many cases, stubbornly refuses to state the truth.

Ask yourself this... just how disdainful of the American people does Barack Obama have to be, to actually do things like this? *Ask yourself...*

Clearly, Obama has had an agenda of favoritism towards Muslim nations and Islam itself since he was elected in 2008. When he arranged that June 2009 Cairo apology speech it was reported that he requested that the leaders of the Muslim Brotherhood (the grandfather of all of the Islamic terrorist organizations) be seated front and center in the audience. *Why?*

Here at home, to make matters worse, as Muslims enter our country those of them that are radicalized or that are Jihadists will be harder to keep track of because the Obama Administration has put limitations on law enforcement officials by disallowing profiling and imposing time limits on just how long suspicious persons can be investigated and monitored. This amounts to being prohibited from describing threatening individuals, whether they are Muslim Jihadists, other terror suspects, or criminals in general. This is stupidity and recklessness beyond belief. Yet it is the policy being forced on our national security officials and even on our local law enforcement by Barack Obama and his administration.

In addition to that stupidity, there is also his directive to the FBI prohibiting that agency from conducting surveillance on Mosques in America. This is also idiocy. Is it part of an agenda...? Unless one thinks Barack Obama to be a moron, or a buffoon, which I do not; then these actions on his part are most certainly going to raise obvious questions as to his real motives: and more importantly; his allegiances. They are obviously not motives and allegiances that put America and Americans first. *So once again: why...?*

If all of these policies, which put Americans at risk, are not enough we are all subjected to Barack Obama's insulting lectures in which he pontificates to us about a backlash against Muslims. What backlash, Mr. President? Even after 911 there was no backlash of any significance.

All of Barack Obama's policies with regard to the Muslim faith and many of his statements clearly show a bias in favor of Islam that extends beyond just being fair to that religion. To many, Obama's policies in terms of fighting Islamic radicals in the Middle-East and his refusal to use more force there to quell the growth of those Islamic radical forces appear to be timid or just not militarily smart. But... if you couple Obama's timid war on terror strategies with his refusal to hit the ISIS terrorists harder and then even to call those terrorists Islamic, and his prohibition from imposing more stringent security measures on suspicious Muslims in the U.S., you come up with a different picture. It is a picture, which reveals that there seems to be a very deliberate protectionism for Islam that is being imposed on America by Barack Obama, as opposed to his ineptitude or timidity.

Is this conspiratorial? Are Obama's actions and policies part of an agenda of his that he hasn't told us about? Has he made a deal with the devil? Or had he made his deal with the devil before he even took office? Perhaps that's why he went to Cairo and addressed Muslim leaders so soon after taking office in 2009 and apologized for America. Well, we may never know the truth and none of us can read his mind…

We can however, look at his actions. What follows is just a short list of some of the measures, policies and directives that have been issued and are being enforced by Barack Obama concerning Islam and the threat from Islamic extremists, both abroad and here at home. Maybe we can glean what his motives really are from these; his own directives, his own policies and his own statements. Remember the old adage? If it walks like a duck and talks like a duck…

After reading this list see what conclusions you come to.

2009 - Obama's apology tour in 2009 culminated with his infamous Cairo speech in which he addressed the leaders of the Middle Eastern Muslim world and the leaders of the Muslim Brotherhood and blamed heightened tensions between Muslims and the U.S. on "American Colonialism" which, he said, deprived Muslims of opportunities.

Just a note: *The United States has never occupied or colonized any middle-eastern countries. European countries did, but not America. Even during and after the Iraq War, America did not take that country's oil or force the Iraqi's to pay for any of the costs of that war to liberate their country.*

2009 – The Fort Hood massacre. This terrorist attack was completely denied by Barrack Obama and his administration, instead labeling it as an act of "workplace violence." For the next six and a half years the administration continued to deny that this attack was an act of Islamic terrorism. As a consequence of their categorizing it as workplace violence the victims of that attack were denied crucial benefits that were due to them.

2009 - Forcing the Department of Homeland Security to *delete* the names of Muslims in the U.S. with ties to the Muslim Brotherhood from their security databases and the prohibition of surveillance of Mosques by any of the law enforcement agencies in the U.S. (including the FBI).

2010 – In June 2010 a revolt by the citizens of Iran began after a rigged election, which served to re-elect the hard line Muslim regime there. The people of Iran wanted to be free from Muslim extremism in their country. They wanted a more modern government not strictly ruled by hard-line Muslim clerics. They were out in the streets with crowds of protesters that numbered in the millions in their major cities, including their capitol of Tehran. During their protests they could be heard pleading with Obama for support. They kept asking Barack Obama and the U.S. for support for their revolution. Their answer: silence.

Add to these revelatory incidents Barack Obama's announcements to the world (and our enemies) of our military's withdrawal dates from both Iraq and Afghanistan, unrealistic rules of engagement imposed on our troops in those theaters, failure to leave a contingency force behind in Iraq to keep the country stable and out of the hands of radical Islamists, drastic reductions to America's military, the notorious Iran Nuclear Deal and now the forced importation of untold thousands of un-vetted refugees from the Middle-East in opposition to the warnings of his own security officials and in spite of the fact that Obama's own Department of Justice recently reported that of the 580 terrorists that have been prosecuted and convicted in the United States since 2001: 380 were foreign born and 40 others were refugees. That means that of these individuals more than 72% were born on foreign soil and then brought here.

The above statistics by themselves should be a good enough reason to halt the importation of immigrants or refugees whose backgrounds cannot be thoroughly checked and vetted.

It doesn't appear that these policies of Obama were instituted simply to protect Muslims from being offended. Instead these policies seem very much more designed to tie the hands of our military and law enforcement agencies, give information to the Muslim extremists we are fighting and, in the case of Iran; enable them to acquire nuclear weaponry unimpeded and much more quickly.

So, what's really going on here? It seems as if someone is deliberately leveling the playing field for the Islamic Extremists and Muslim hardliners. These people, by the way, are ENEMIES of the United States by their own admission.

Critics of the suppositions made here will of course say that none of these theories can be substantiated. Without an admission from Obama, or his lieutenants, maybe not: but the policies that Barack Obama has instituted already, and the statements he's made defy logic or any modicum of reason; unless of course, he does have another agenda: an agenda that does not have America's interests as its primary purpose. Considering all of the preceding facts reasonable people need to ask themselves why a U.S. president would deliberately do so many things that were harmful and posed such risks to his country and its citizens?

Indeed, we should all ask ourselves that question.

Now Barack Obama has just extended **Temporary Extended Status to all Syrian refugees,** which means that there are no limits as to how many can come here and settle permanently. And don't forget that Homeland Security and law enforcement will not be privy to their locations once they're in this country because of Barack Obama's orders.

Recently, it was learned that Barack Obama surreptitiously transferred $400 million in cash on an unmarked plane to Iran. This cash however, was not made up of United States legal tender. No, it was in other currencies because to use U.S. currency or to electronically transfer these funds would have been against the law. *Enough said…*

****

Unfortunately, on top of all of this, there are other issues to be very leery about concerning what Obama will do in this, his last year in office.

The Control of the Internet

Barack Obama intends on turning over the control of the Internet to the U.N.

Ask yourself why…

Why the need to turn over the control of something that The United States invented, works better than ever imagined and that The United States has willingly shared with the world. All other countries in the world have always been able to use the web without any interference from our government. So, Mr. Obama, why turn it over to foreigners? What's the need? Better yet, what is your motivation for doing this?

Is this just another of Obama's steps to undermine the United States? Ask yourself...

An issue all freedom loving Americans should worry about is Obama's increasing use of executive orders, executive memos (the same thing as executive orders) and out of control issuance of federal regulations by the federal agencies under his direction, (which become de facto federal laws). He has stepped this up dramatically. As he said he would, he's leaving it all on the field: *just in case he can't remain in office...*

Now these regulations (with threats attached to them for those who fail to **immediately** comply) even involve things like invasions to your safety and privacy as well as that of your children: *Like Obama's Bathroom Edict.*

Expect more and more infringements on your rights and freedoms to be imposed on you by Barack Obama and the Democratic Party: Especially while he's still in office.

Many of these measures that will be foisted upon us will cause outrage, yes. But MORE IMPORTANTLY, they will take our attention off the things that the democrats and liberals are doing to accomplish the goals of their overall strategy; to undermine, weaken and then strangle Constitutional freedoms in The United States, bring down capitalism, usher in socialism and finally; to hand over America's sovereignty to *International law and governance.* This is really what it's all about. With regard to Obama himself, though: it appears to be more than that. *There appears to be something more at play in him: something very sinister.*

Barack Obama and The Democratic Party are following and putting life to the rules set out by the anti-American 60's radical and Marxist Saul Alinsky on how to effect changes in a society. In Alinsky's case this is just "code" for how to overthrow American society.

26

Just as an aside, Hillary Clinton was an ardent admirer of Saul Alinsky and was on a first name basis with him when he was alive. She also met with him often. She even wrote her college thesis about him. She was a big fan.

However, in Obama's case it is not just changing American society that he's interested in. From any fair examination of his actions in office one would have to conclude that his agenda reaches far beyond that. His actions appear to reveal motives that have more to do with inflicting harm on America and taking it down, rather than changing it: or "transforming" it as he had put it when running for the presidency.

For example: his fomenting racial strife at every opportunityand causing racial tension is not transforming anything for the betterment of the country. And reducing security measures in the U.S., which are designed to prevent terrorism, is also not very transformational. These are all things designed to do something else.

Below is the list of Saul Alinsky's *8 Levels of Control*. See if you don't agree that the Democratic Party, Barack Obama and now, Hillary Clinton have been employing Alinsky's tactics and strategies to disrupt America, cause discontentment, strip people of their rights and drastically change this country.

You will quickly recognize these tactics as those that have been employed by Barack Obama with the full endorsement of both Hillary Rodham Clinton and their new, far-left Democratic Party.

The 8 Levels of Control by the Marxist radical Saul Alinsky: taken from his book Rules for Radicals.

1)Healthcare

Control healthcare and you control the people.

2)Poverty

Increase the Poverty level as high as possible, poor people are easier to control and will not fight back if you are providing everything for them to live.

3) Debt

Increase the debt to an unsustainable level. That way you are able to increase taxes, and this will produce more poverty.

4) Gun Control

Remove the ability to defend themselves from the Government. That way you are able to create a police state.

5) Welfare

Take control of every aspect of their lives (Food, Housing, and Income)

6) Education

Take control of what people read and listen to – take control of what children learn in school.

7) Religion

Remove the belief in the God from the Government and schools.

8) Class Warfare

Divide the people into the wealthy and the poor. This will cause more discontent and it will be easier to take tax the wealthy with the support of the poor. This last step is actually is actually spelled out in Hillary Clinton's campaign platform.

Alinsky was an agitator and Marxist bent on bringing down America. He is an icon of liberals, Hillary Clinton, Barack Obama and the Democratic Party.

One final note about Saul Alinsky: he is considered to be the very first modern-day "community organizer." The term ring a bell...?

As if all of the problems previously outlined are not overwhelming enough it has been reported by credible sources that the federal government is now hording guns and ammunition and issuing firearms to employees in agencies that have nothing to do with security or law enforcement, such as: The IRS, the Department of Health and Human Services and many others.

Before 2009 about 100,000 federal employees had government issued firearms. But since Obama's been in office that number has increased to over 240,000 (more than the entire U.S. Marine Corps). So this number has more than doubled since Barack Obama has been in office.

Ask yourself why...

In addition to the issuance of these firearms to government employees that have NO BUSINESS having them, the government is also reported to be hording tons of ammunition: allegedly more than 4 billion rounds already stockpiled by the non-essential government agencies. *Why?*

There is absolutely no reason for employees of these agencies to have firearms. So... what could that reason be?

****

So, what else will he do?

Barack Obama has deliberately hurt America in every way he can up to now, but he is not done: far from it. In this, his last six months, he is proving to be more dangerous and aggressively anti-American than ever. In Obama's last three months we can expect him to be even more extreme than that. As I have mentioned already: he said it himself; he's going to leave it all on the field. No holds barred...

The worst possible outcome could very well be that he will actually impose martial law if anything goes wrong for Hillary. At that point he will be free to override Americans' Second Amendment Rights to own firearms, start gun confiscations and then also suspend many other rights guaranteed by our Constitution. He would also be free to expand federal government controls over everyone and everything in our society. In short: ALL the necessities of life could then be controlled by the federal government: *a socialist's dream.*

This might seem far-fetched: but is it really? Consider that we're talking about Barack Obama: the most flagrantly audacious individual ever to hold the office of president.

Add to these nightmares that he would be free to eliminate the country's borders, allow open and unimpeded immigration and that he could flood this country with completely UN-VETTED Muslim refugees.

By the way… if things go right for Hillary and she is elected: except for martial law; she fully intends to do almost everything above. That would be Hillary's new America.

In the event that Hillary stays well and gets elected it still will not bode well for Americans. Obama will still have three months to carry on his campaign to undermine America. Don't expect Hillary to do anything to impede his efforts because she agrees with him. Hillary is a socialist and globalist with no particular allegiance to America; save to exploit it, which she has done her entire life.

We can also expect that the number of un-vetted Syrian and Muslim refugees brought here by Obama will be higher than what has been announced by him: probably very much higher.

And, we should also expect a flood of new federal regulations, putting controls on energy and related industries and the further strangulation of private and small businesses.

Finally, we should also expect Obama's Administration to take over more of our cities' police departments and impose policies on these law enforcement agencies that will make everyone less safe and encourage the crime problem in this country even further.

****

TWO

Domestic Security, Tranquility and Race Relations

Domestic security and tranquility involves more than just protecting U.S. citizens from terrorist attacks. As was already discussed, Obama is indeed imposing unwarranted threats on the safety of Americans by relaxing the scrutiny of suspicious Muslims here and by bringing in un-vetted Muslim refugees whose backgrounds and affiliations are unknown, and he's doing this on a fast track. But there are many other issues to be considered as well.

Domestic security and tranquility also involve national crime, race relations, economic conditions and even class and gender warfare, all of which have been inflamed and made worse by the Obama Administration. Suffice it to say that Barack Obama has incited more friction and tension in everyone of these areas than any president in memory.

At least with respect to race relations, Barack Obama, as the country's first president of color could have made great strides in healing divisions between different racial groups in The United States. Instead, he has inflamed and made worse, every situation that arose that contained any racial element at all. Even in situations where issues of race were not at issue: he needlessly infused race into them, thereby causing great detriment to race relations in this country. Now race relations have deteriorated back to where they were in the late 1960's.

Barack Obama inherited a nation with crime in decline and at the lowest levels in decades. Likewise, he inherited a nation with less racial tension than any time in memory. However, he will leave office with crime rising very fast and with race relations in shambles.

Crime, of course, affects all of our safety and that of our children and family members. So, when a president says or does things that serve to incite more crime it affects us all. And unfortunately, President Obama has repeatedly said and done things that have inflamed the feelings of blacks by stating that they were deliberately being unfairly discriminated against by American law enforcement. (Implied here by him is that it is of course, "white" cops doing the discriminating against minorities: and in particular, African-Americans). In so doing, this president has tacitly given legitimization for more criminal behavior on the part of those minorities: especially black Americans.

31

Barack Obama's prejudicial, inflammatory and largely unfounded claims along these lines are always seen by him through a racial prism. A prism so tightly embraced by him that it blinds him from accepting the facts about crime in this country. Or perhaps his bias is such that he will only lay blame for crime at the feet of white Americans, while totally ignoring the facts.

The facts are that while only 13% of the population, African-Americans commit the majority of murders in this country (over 50%). And, of that 13% population group, those actually committing the violent crimes are predominantly males: representing approximately 6% of the population.

This crime data, by the way, comes from Barack Obama's own (DOJ) Department of Justice, which has been run by African-Americans since he's been in office.

Barack Obama also ignores the fact that the majority of these crimes are being committed by people using un-registered guns and NOT by people with LEGALLY REGISTERED guns. The lawful gun owners in America are not committing all these crimes: either black or white. The extremely high crime rates of blacks are also true for armed robberies, car-jackings, home invasions, rapes and most other violent crimes.

The facts are that blacks do commit more than 50% of the murders in The United States with whites and light skinned Hispanics being accountable for most of the rest of the murders. Murders by whites account for ten percent of murders nationally.

According to Larry Elder (a nationally syndicated radio talk show host who is himself an African-American) whites commit just ten percent (10%) of the murders in this country: even though they comprise over 70% of the overall population.

According to the 2010 U.S. Census whites were 72.4% of the population at that time.

Insofar as police deliberately targeting African-Americans: the statistics do not bear this out. In her newly released book, "The War On Cops" Heather Mac Donald sites the real facts and statistics about police interactions with blacks. It is notable that all of the shootings of blacks by police do not even comprise *one percent* of black homicide deaths in this country. It is also noteworthy that black males commit violent crimes at a rate 8 times higher than white males do, so interactions between the police and black males is obviously going to be higher than with other racial groups.

Additionally, black teenagers commit homicides 11 times more than White and Hispanic teenagers combined and 18 times more than the number of homicides committed by just white teens. These are the reasons for so much interaction with young black males. They are committing much more of the murders and the other violent gun crimes: So much for targeting blacks.

It is a fact that many more white people are killed by the police than are blacks in this country: more than twice as many whites are killed by the police as blacks in the U.S.; even though blacks are committing many more times the number of violent crimes.

No part of the truth, it seems, matters to Barack Obama.

Obama has never addressed, in any meaningful way, the rampant crime being committed by black Americans in our cities and particularly the outrageous violent crime in the black neighborhoods of Chicago (his own home town).

In the seven and a half years that Obama has been president there have been close to 3,500 murders in Chicago, dwarfing the statistics in all our other cities. Yet he ignores the wholesale murder going on there and instead tries to make it harder for law-abiding citizens to own a firearm, which is their right.

By the way: Chicago has some of the strictest gun laws in the entire country.

Obama also ignores the fact that, for the most part, the guns used to commit all these murders are NOT REGISTERED GUNS so more gun laws will do absolutely nothing to prevent these homicides.

To my knowledge Barack Obama has never even gone to those Chicago neighborhoods to speak. Nor did he ever send Eric Holder there while he was his Attorney General. Nor did he give any national addresses about it and he doesn't address the crime there in his weekly radio addresses even though the murder rates there every weekend are stupendous and worse than ever. You have to ask yourself why?

Yes, ask yourself... Is he more interested in reducing murders; or stripping away gun rights from law abiding citizens? Ask yourself...

Instead of accepting the facts for what they are Obama makes statements that put the blame on the police: insinuating that it is the police that are the problem and not the criminals themselves; at least not criminals who happen to be black Americans. President Obama appears to be formulating his conclusions based upon his own racial prejudice and then makes these false assertions based on those racial biases as well. There are many examples of this bias. Below are but a few.

He over-reacted in the Massachusetts Skip Gates incident in his first term, then likewise with the Travon Martin incident, then with the Ferguson incident with Michael Brown, then Baltimore and so on. In each of these incidents he was wrong, acted prematurely in a bigoted and partisan way before he even knew the facts related to those situations.

Barack Obama's impetuous statements actually fueled the violent rioting in Ferguson. This is not to mention the fact that he destroyed the life of an innocent police officer (Darren Wilson) and made a martyr of Michael Brown who was nothing more than a violent thug.

Even after his own DOJ (Department of Justice) and the FBI swarmed into Ferguson and exhaustively investigated the death of Michael Brown and found that the shooting of Brown by Officer Darren Wilson was justified, Obama wouldn't change his position! No apologies... not even a word.

This is not rational behavior. And it's certainly not judicious behavior. It is the behavior of a man with a particular political-racial vent that he is acting upon in spite of irrefutable facts. It is the behavior of a man with an ax to grind. And, it appears to be a racially motivated ax. With his untruthful and incendiary statements President Barack Obama has been fomenting anarchy. *Saul Alinsky would be proud...*

Barack Obama makes sweeping statements about the police and criminal justice system, charging them with purposely discriminating against blacks and disproportionately targeting them, prosecuting them and incarcerating them.

It doesn't seem to occur to Mr. Obama that it is *other black people* that are calling the police about these black criminals in the first place. They are the ones that are making the 911 calls to the police. And it happens to be other blacks that are identifying these black criminals as the offenders.

No, Mr. Obama... this is not discrimination. This is criminality at epidemic levels on the part of males of a particular racial group. This is what needs to be addressed – not the criminal justice system.

This rampant criminality puts Americans of every stripe, in all areas of the country, at risk. But, it affects the African American citizens' neighborhoods most of all: as evidenced by the murder rates in those black communities.

Mr. Obama might want to take note of the fact that the enormous increase in violent crime and murder rates started spiking IMMEDIATELY after his and Eric Holder's statements and actions concerning Ferguson, Missouri. Prior to that, for two decades, the crime rates across America had been in dramatic decline; largely due to proactive policing which, Obama and his administration now have labeled as discriminatory: towards minorities of course.

Perhaps; just perhaps, it would be wiser and more productive to face up to the facts about black crime and do something about all of the illegal guns in this population group since, in fact, they are committing the majority of the violent crime in this country.

Perhaps, just perhaps, it would be more productive to send the swarms of federal investigators (as Obama and Holder did in Ferguson) into these inner city neighborhoods to find out why these young black men are so highly disposed towards violent crime. And... perhaps, just perhaps, Barack Obama might want to take a look at the "sub-culture" that is breeding this criminal behavior and glorifying, rather than condemning it. Just perhaps...

Barack Obama has not done anything of significance to reduce the levels of homicide in America's African-American inner city communities. Indeed, whether he realizes it or not, his posture and the statements he's made laying blame for the actions of criminal behavior at the feet of law enforcement and

35

the criminal justice system only serve to make the problem of black crime worse. As do the Democratic Party's claims that poverty is the contributing factor for the high incidence of violent crimes being committed by African-Americans. Poverty may be responsible for some of the crime. It can lead one to steal. But, it does not lead one to murder.

And, in fact, the crime rates during the 2008-09 recession were the lowest in many decades: even among blacks.

Barck Obama, Hillary Clinton and the Democratic Party are now on another campaign to take guns away from legal gun owners in The United States, but they have done literally nothing about the illegal guns in the inner cities in primarily black neighborhoods across America. In fact, they don't seem to be addressing the high crime in these areas at all. *Why?*

Obama's continual incendiary and false statements which serve to validate resentments among blacks about police and criminal justice's discrimination towards them have fueled an epidemic of attacks against police, dramatic increases in already epidemic levels of black crime, and led to incidents like the attacks in Dallas recently. Then, at the memorial service for the fallen police officers, Barack Obama went on to politicize things and, once again, lecture white Americans about racism in America.

Ironically, none of Obama's comments were relevant to what happened in Dallas at all, since the shooter there was a black man that had stated that he wanted to kill white people and, white cops, in particular. Not once was this mentioned. Instead, Obama used this painful and solemn occasion to lecture white Americans. Perhaps he should be made aware that racism works both ways and that HE, Barack Obama, is the perfect example of this.

Under Barack Obama's watch American race relations have deteriorated to the condition they were at in the late 1960's and 1970's. This is frightening. His continual practice of infusing his racial bigotry into any incidents that occur between law enforcement and blacks, and then, making inappropriate and incendiary remarks without even bothering to wait for the facts of these cases to come to light has done incalculable damage to race relations.

Obama is actually instigating racial hatred, division and violence. It is hard to believe that he could be so unwise as to think that his statements are not stoking the flames of racial hatred. Instead, from his statements and actions it appears as if he's deliberately trying to create racial strife in this country. And indeed, he is doing just that. Barack Obama bears the lion's share of responsibility for the continual attacks on police and the violence being perpetrated by groups such as Black Lives Matter and also for the escalating crime wave in black communities in America: not to mention the executions of police officers across the country.

Barack Obama, Hillary Clinton and the mainstream media have continually omitted reporting the truth about the incidents of black men being killed in confrontations with police in this country. According to Larry Elder and Sheriff David Clarke of Milwaukee (both prominent African – Americans) that truth is that in the vast majority of instances, the individuals who were killed in these confrontations deliberately failed to comply with lawful police commands and physically resisted arrest or detainment.

Yes, there are incidents where blacks are unjustly shot by police and they should be dealt with harshly: BUT LEGALLY. However, in the majority of these controversial cases it is the black individual who raises the ante in a confrontation and not the police officer. Those are the facts.

Once again, we see that the facts don't matter. Only Barack Obama's false narrative that America is still a racist country matters.

Based on the actual facts, ask yourself: Who is the REAL racist here?

Worse yet, all of Obama's statements and allegations are based on non-existent data, lies and his own prejudice. These false statements he makes are, of course, in keeping with the lies about black criminality, which are consistently told by the Democratic Party, the mainstream media and now, of course, Hillary Clinton, too.

Immediately after the shootings of the five Dallas police officers Hillary began announcing to America's African-American community that she was going to get white Americans to change the way they think about the plight of African-Americans' being discriminated against, and victimized by, white police officers.

After the Baltimore incident in which Freddie Gray died while in police custody Hillary immediately condemned the six police officers involved. Since then of course, a judge, who is himself a black man, has found these officers to be innocent of the charges brought by the race-baiting District Attorney, Marilyn Mosby.

At an address given to the NAACP Hillary Clinton pandered to her audience by telling outright lies (quoting false statistics, etc.) about the police. It is so sickening to see that this mendacious and unscrupulous woman will just say anything to get black votes, regardless of the detriment that it will cause to blacks themselves or the country as a whole.

Hillary goes so far as to endorse Black Lives Matter and legitimize the claims of this notorious organization. But she really went too far when she had the mothers of Michael Brown and Freddie Gray at the Democratic National Convention and portrayed them as grieving mothers of "children" who had been unjustly killed by the police.

Hillary has given legitimacy to the out and out lies being told about the death of Michael Brown in Ferguson, Missouri. By doing this she too is guilty of fomenting racism and violence in this country. She knows very well the truth about Ferguson and yet she chooses to propagate racially motivated lies instead.

Ask yourself why...

Let me help you: she does it for votes. The truth doesn't matter. If she has to lie to get those votes - she will. The harm caused by her position doesn't matter. At least not to her.

Barack Obama's reckless lies about black criminality and the responsibility for it are malicious, extremely destructive and serve no productive purpose. His recent disdainful and untruthful statements that America has a long way to go in terms of race relations are equally detrimental to improving such relations. What he is doing instead, is stoking the flames of racism in the black communities across America.

Is this by design? Ask yourself...

We have only seen the beginnings of the damage this president has done and will continue to do along these lines. Despite his egotistical claims: in terms of race relations Barack Obama has proven himself to be the worst president in American history: with the possible exception of Jefferson Davis.

During a recent national radio interview Heather Mac Donald was asked by radio host Rush Limbaugh if there was anything that she could think of that would help to bring down the high black crime rates; especially in the black communities.

*Heather Mac Donald replied that America should try something **totally new**. What was that new thing, you might ask.*

It was to, for once, TELL THE TRUTH about the reasons for the high crime being committed by African-Americans in The United States.

****

In 2012, during Obama's re-election campaign, we all saw the Democratic Party's "War on Women" strategy employed relentlessly. To the extent that a war on women exists: which it doesn't; the Democrats grossly overstated disparities on wages between men and women; misquoting studies, etc. The point isn't even the argument that it does or doesn't exist. The real issue is that, once again, the Democrats were using false facts to cause divisiveness: in this case between genders.

Radical feminism has been a cause celebre since the 1970's. This extreme form of feminism is built upon hate and fomenting hate is something that the liberals have used to their advantage for decades: all too often, successfully. And, of course, the liberal media was all too happy to reinforce the false narrative of the Democrats along these lines both in 2008 and again in 2012. They will do so again this year. And Hillary Clinton will exploit this to the fullest: when in fact she has been abusive and hostile towards women who came forward alleging that they had been accosted and even raped by her husband Bill Clinton.

She has also taken huge amounts of money from Mid-Eastern countries, like Saudi Arabia, that discriminate against women to the point of persecuting them. What has she done for the women of those countries? *Ask yourself...*

****

THREE

Open Borders, Lawlessness and Public Safety

The Democratic Party's continuing policy of "Open Borders" is often blamed on Republicans who want cheap labor. Nonsense. Republicans do not want open borders: period. Perhaps there are some businesses that may want the cheap labor, but to the extent that that may be true, those businesses are not just Republican owned businesses: they are owned by Democrats as well and those motives don't begin to approach the nefarious reasons that the Democratic Party wants to keep the borders open.

It has been a Democratic Party strategy for decades to flood the country with illegal immigrants and then, through constant pressure, give them the right to vote: even though, constitutionally, they are not allowed to vote unless they have become citizens.

After seven years of Obama's rule (yes, I said rule) we now see this strategy coming to fruition. The governor of California has recently signed a bill giving all of the illegal aliens in that state the right to vote. Expect other Democratic controlled states to immediately follow suit.

And by the way: there are more than eleven million illegal immigrants in California alone.

The Democrats, and in particular Barack Obama, have no use for the U.S. Constitution. They are doing everything they can do to undermine it right now. To them it is an impediment to changing America into a socialist country run by elites, which of course, they consider themselves to be.

Aside from the obvious political implications, which will be disastrous, there are grave public safety issues involved in this destruction of America's sovereignty as well. No one considers these associated risks right now, but we are indeed, already suffering from them.

Tuberculosis, polio and other life threatening diseases, which had been eradicated in The United States long ago, have now been re-introduced to the country. And don't think for a moment that health officials will catch the individuals carrying these illnesses: They won't and THEY ARE NOT.

As if the problem weren't bad enough with the flood of illegal immigrants on the southern border, Barack Obama is already bringing in a flood of Muslim immigrants from Syria, many of whom are tubercular. And, no one is checking these people at all.

And it is not just diseases that we are at risk from: this unchecked flow of immigrants has also brought a huge surge of crime with it. A HUGE SURGE.

Over 640,000 violent crimes have been committed by illegals in Texas alone during Obama's term in office. That's 640,000 home invasions, kidnappings, robberies, rapes and murders. In just one state! That is a lot of crime. Don't think for a minute, though, that this problem is just a Texas problem: it's not.

Violent crimes like murders, rapes, armed robberies, home invasions and car jackings are being committed at an alarming rate by illegals and, at a rate MUCH HIGHER THAN THAT OF AMERICAN CITIZENS.

The Border patrol has reported that it has been ordered by the Obama Adminstration not to arrest illegals, and… not even to make them sign the notice to appear forms that are required, or even to check them for valid ID's. The United States has the distinction of having completely open borders in the world today. Why? *Yes, ask yourself…*

*It has been recently reported on cable news that more than 1,000,000 illegal aliens have ignored their deportation orders and **over 170,000 of them happen to be convicted criminals!***

Along with this it was further reported that the Obama Administration has been lying about the number of crimes actually being committed by illegals.

Obama's illegal amnesty, which is still going forward despite the Federal Court rulings which ordered the Administration to stop it, was done to give the Progressives and Democrats millions of new Democratic voters. But, they will not be, and are not, satisfied with that. They want a numerical voting advantage that will make it impossible for conservative candidates to win elections and thus achieve total and perpetual control over the country.

At that point there would never be another conservative president or conservative representatives of any kind. And we will finally become the totalitarian, socialist country that the Democrats want.

And finally, add to all these risks the possibility of terrorists coming in through the open southern border. Yes, that is happening too. At least according to the Border Patrol and the Sheriffs of the border counties. They have been on television warning us of the dangers posed to all Americans. Decide for yourself who you believe: the law enforcement officials who are there... or Barack Obama.

Obama has grown so brazen now that he doesn't care what the courts say and he certainly isn't worried about our Republican controlled Congress. The "establishment" Republicans repeatedly show themselves to be either cowards or traitors who are going along with these progressive socialist policies. It really doesn't matter which of the two they are: the destruction of our country will be the same.

But, it appears, that Barack Obama might even have an additional motive for flooding the country with all of these immigrants. Could this have something to do with making white Americans who were born here a "minority" in The United States? *Ask yourself...*

Adding fuel to the fire in terms of the immigration problems, Hillary Clinton has announced that she will completely eliminate all of the U.S. borders and declare an amnesty to those that have already come here illegally within the first 100 days of her administration if she is elected president.

These measures will serve to beckon immigrants here from Mexico, Central America and South America by the tens of millions and flood this country with low or unskilled skilled people, many of whom will be dependent on the state for support. Her announcements will also be an open invitation to the criminal elements from all of those countries.

Hillary's plans to expand welfare with no questions asked will, of course, include all of these people: All tens of millions of them. Her answer to the financial burden they will cause to Americans: **raise taxes.**

****

FOUR

Foreign Policy, the War On Terror and National Security

In June of 2009 there were mass demonstrations throughout Iran, in its capital, Tehran and most of the other cities throughout that country. The people were protesting the hard line, Islamic regime and rigged elections that had just occurred there, which kept that strict Islamic regime in power. At the time Barack Obama had a fantastic, once in a lifetime, opportunity to endorse that country's largely moderate population that was protesting the rigged elections and continuation of the regime. Indeed, there were millions of Iranians in the streets chanting, "Obama, will you back us?" There was a revolution starting. The people of Iran were demanding a more moderate government. And they wanted the support of America: if nothing else; at least in spirit. They wanted President Obama to speak out on their behalf. They truly expected America's support.

But, Barack Obama offered no support whatsoever. Instead he supported the hard-line Islamic regime that had been in power since 1979. During these protests thousands of Iranians were imprisoned and scores were murdered in the streets by the repressive government. Soon enough, with no support, the nascent revolution was over.

One has to wonder why Barack Obama didn't even lend verbal support to the people of Iran, who clearly wanted to be free of the shackles of their oppressive government. And one also has to wonder what would have happened after that in the Mid-East had Iran, the largest Islamic nation in that region of the world, taken a step towards moderation and freedom. Would it have led to a relaxation of the tensions between Islamic radicals and the west and our country?

Barack Obama didn't offer support to Iran then, but he has now. He has now because Iran is firmly back in the hands of the Muslim Brotherhood. So Obama has given Iran an agreement, which affords that country's radical Islamic regime a quicker way to acquire nuclear weapons and 150 billion (actually 170 billion now) dollars to do this with. Obama's agreement with Iran was done against the vehement advice of our military leaders, most of Obama's foreign policy advisors and against the protests of our staunchest ally in the mid-east and the ONLY democracy there: Israel.

Iran's current regime might have developed nuclear weapons in the future anyway, but the actions of Barack Obama **ensured** that it will get them: and his lopsided agreement also **ensured** that it will have them sooner, rather than later.

Hillary added to the risks of an Iran with nuclear capability by approving a deal that allowed Russian entities to get control of 20 percent of the uranium reserves of the U.S. when she was Secretary of State.

Think of it: Iran with nuclear weapons; Iran happens to be the largest sponsor of Islamic terrorism in the world!

So, as it turned out: Barack Obama gave them the money and Hillary gave them the fuel for nuclear weapons.

At the time that the Iran Nuclear Deal was announced the current Secretary of State, John Kerry, publicly stated that Iran will most probably use a good part of the money Obama is sending to Iran to sponsor terrorism!

On July 18th the Associated Press (definitely NOT a conservative news organization) reported that secret, unpublicized parts of Obama's Iran Nuclear Deal will actually allow, and thus enable, Iran to develop nuclear weapons in **half the time that was told to us by the Barack Obama Administration.**

We should all ask ourselves if these are the actions of a man who puts America's security first: Or the security of western civilization, for that matter. It all seems to favor Islam and radical Islam at that. Once again, we need to question where Barack Obama's allegiances lie. It doesn't seem as though they're with us.

And while we're at it we should all be asking the very same question of Hillary Rodham Clinton.

In addition to what Barack Obama has accomplished (I say accomplished because Iran was clearly by his intent – not by mistake) with regard to Iran one has only to look at Obama's other actions in the Middle East to get a clearer picture of his "big picture" and his agenda.

He and Hillary Clinton (it was reported to be her idea) engineered what turned out to be the Libyan disaster. Long before 2009 Libya had been subdued. Muammar Quaddaffi, the country's leader had gotten rid of any of his sophisticated weapons and was being civil. There was absolutely no reason to oust him. But Clinton and Obama did just that by supplying arms to rebels opposing Quaddaffi there and instigating trouble designed to overthrow him.

Why Quaddaffi? Neither Hillary Clinton nor Barack Obama has ever given a plausible reason for their interference in Libya. So what was the reason? Probably it was that Quaddaffi presented an easy target for Hillary Clinton to have a foreign policy coup: literally. Here was a small country, with a formerly despotic leader, who had a past connected with a notorious terrorist incident, but that was now peaceful (considering the standards of the region he's in) and that would be easy pickings.

This coup in Libya could be a feather in Hillary's cap and would be something she could tout in her upcoming run for the presidency. Yes, of course, this smacks of an arrangement between Hillary and Obama. Hillary had stepped aside in 2008 (because she was beaten by Obama and the Democratic Party threw her overboard). She had then been appointed as Secretary of State to give her the foreign policy credentials she would need to run for the presidency and succeed Obama in 2016.

The problem with their planning with regard to Libya was that there wasn't any. Instead of anticipating that they would need a replacement government that would be friendly to the west and continue Quaddaffi's more peaceful posture, Hillary and Obama left Libya wide open for a takeover. And they got one: by ISIS. Libya quickly became ISIS Central and a safe haven for ISIS's training grounds: replete with modern weaponry; compliments of Hillary Clinton.

Within months radicals from all over the Mid-East were pouring into Libya, anxious to enlist in the new terrorist organization. Hillary's authorization to send huge quantities of sophisticated land weapons to aid the Libyan rebels in their efforts to oust the old Libyan leader had put the ISIS radicals on steroids. Hillary was responsible for that fiasco because she had not given any thought to controlling who got the weapons once they arrived in Libya. When those rebels turned out to be ISIS it was too late: the toothpaste was out of the tube.

This staged coup was supposed to be the modern template for all modern governments to follow. As soon as Quaddaffi was ousted Hillary Clinton's (unlawful) aide, Sydney Blumenthal even sent her congratulatory emails that regaled her for her superior foreign policy talents, citing that she should immediately take an "International Bow" for her masterfully executed plan. He went so far as to say that the goddess of history (Cleo) was watching Hillary. The idea was to show how her superior intellect could accomplish the overthrow of a dictator without the use of force and boots on the ground and free that country's population to pursue freedom for themselves.

Of course, Hillary's supporters conveniently left out the fact that she did indeed need boots on the ground: it's just that they weren't American boots. They were local boots and those boots failed. The arms then fell into the hands of the ISIS rebels and the ISIS VARSITY TEAM took the field: armed to the teeth.

And, of course, this created the need for a hasty cover story so that the folly of Hillary's plan and the fact that she had gotten Obama to sign off on it would not be seen as the reason for the calamity. Obama was campaigning for his re-election and had been bragging that terrorism was defeated and that the war on terrorism was almost won. The election was around the corner: the timing couldn't have been worse.

Hillary Clinton is campaigning on the strength of her experience in foreign policy. Her Libya fiasco is an actual example of her experience: So much for Hillary Clinton's foreign policy acumen.

There were plenty of internal problems in Libya but there was not an imminent threat of any organized terrorist presence that country. Libyan leader Muammar Quaddaffi simply diddn't tolerate terrorist organizations of any size or strength in his country because he wanted no threats to his power and his regime there. Organized terrorist groups could stir up more trouble for him and he already had a disgruntled public that wasn't too happy with him as it was.

At any rate, after this short-sighted ousting the country had that presence: and had it in spades, thanks to the bungling by Hillary Clinton, which was most probably done all for the sake of her self-centered political ambitions.

Then there was Benghazi.

The first thing to understand about the tragedy of Benghazi is that Libyan Ambassador Stevens and his staff had pleaded for additional security there for 9 months prior to the September 11th attacks that took the Ambassador's life and that of 3 other Americans. These pleas were made to the Secretary of State 600 times! That's six hundred desperate requests for help in nine months. Hillary Clinton claims that she was not aware of any of those requests. She didn't know about them? Hillary had obviously insulated herself from critically important situations to a very dangerous degree!

It's funny that donors to the Clinton Foundation were always able to get through to the Secretary of State without any problem.

Maybe Ambassador and his team should have said they were going to make a donation: that would have got them through to Hillary; after all she seemed to always have time for her donors...

To not be aware of 600 desperate requests for help from an Ambassador is beyond outrageous and in the end cost the lives of people that depended on Hillary Clinton for their safety. She was the one responsible for sending help if it was needed. A Secretary of State is also REQUIRED to know the status of her department's people who are in the field: especially when they're in dangerous theaters of operation. After Hillary's fiasco there was no more dangerous place than Libya.

How in the world could this woman be so insulated that she was unaware of 600 requests from an ambassador stationed in one of the most dangerous territories in the world? The answer to that question is all too obvious. She was aware but decided to ignore the requests for help from her team: the team she had sent there; and even left them there to fend for themselves on the night of the attack, which took their lives.

There are other reasons that the dire situation in Libya had to be known by the Secretary of State. After the Libyan leader's removal and public murder the situation in Libya had gotten so dangerous that the British had pulled out and so had the Red Cross. There is absolutely no way that Hillary Clinton, as the Secretary of State, could not have known of the situation there. She had to know of the volatility in Libya and therefore, she most certainly should have known about the desperate requests for added security by her team there. So, the obvious question is, why was this security denied?

Well, in all likelihood, it had more to do with the re-election campaign of Barack Obama and loss of face for Secretary of State Hillary Clinton. Why does that matter? It matters because the election was a mere six weeks away and Obama had just run around the country stating that the terrorists were on their heels and the war on terror was all but over. To have a terrorist eruption at that time didn't fit the narrative being spun by President Obama and the Democratic Party. It certainly wouldn't favor his re-election chances and it made Hillary look like an inept fool.

Barrack Obama and Hillary Clinton had just employed their self-acclaimed and highly touted foreign policy skills and intervened to improve Libya but in the process, opened the door for ISIS and then armed them to the teeth. Libya was in chaos and ISIS had yet another country to occupy.

Hence, the cover-up that followed. And it followed quickly. Even before the incident was over that night Hillary Clinton had come up with the excuse she would use to deflect attention from her own culpability for the tragedy. This convenient excuse turned out to be a Youtube video critical of Islam.

It was reported that these people (Hillary and staffers) were in Washington watching while the attacks were still going on, and, instead of concentrating on how to help the Americans fighting for their lives in Benghazi, searched the Internet for a suitable video to use as a scapegoat: This outrageous lie was then promoted by both Hillary Clinton and the Obama Whitehouse as the reason for the attacks in Benghazi. It was the start of Hillary's coverup.

After Quaddaffi's murder was shown on TV internationally, the snarky Hillary was caught on video proudly bragging, "We came, we saw, he died! Ha, ha, ha, ha."

Perhaps Hillary should have at least waited for the dust to settle a bit before making such a snide and glib comment. Or at least to see what the results of her foreign policy coup would really be.

As for Obama: he also meddled again in the Mid-East, this time in Egypt (there was no valid reason for intervening in the affairs of this country either), replacing a moderate leader with Muhammad Morsi, who was a leading member of the Muslim Brotherhood. Once again, Obama's ties to this notorious organization of hard line extremist Muslims evidenced itself. We know Hillary's reasons for engineering her phony coup: it was pure avarice and lust for power. But WHY was Obama involved in Egypt's affairs in conjunction with the Muslim Brotherhood?

Once again... ask yourself....

Note: *In the two years prior to the replacement of Egypt's Prime Minister with Muhammad Morsi, Barack Obama had stopped the funding which had been provided to pro human rights groups within Egypt for years. Why...?*

After Morsi took over in Egypt Barack Obama sent him a billion dollars of American taxpayers' money and new tanks as well as F-16s.

To put it bluntly: Barack Obama and Hillary Clinton have thrown the Mid-East into chaos. They have aided (whether knowingly or otherwise) anti-American regimes and repeatedly left vacuums of power, which the bad actors have immediately filled. On top of that their lack of foresight (or possibly lack of concern) has left thousands of military vehicles, weapons with munitions and tanks to our enemies: This military equipment is now being used by ISIS against us and our allies.

Funny that Barack Obama would never arm the Kurdish fighters (our only reliable and effective allies in Iraq) yet he lets billions of dollars worth of armaments be taken over by ISIS. Yes, funny... isn't it?

As far as the War On Terror is concerned we have to ask ourselves why it is that this president has always informed our enemies of troop strengths, dates for withdrawals, and even when Special Forces units were being sent into an area with specifics as to their strength, where they would be deployed and when they would arrive. This would seem to be information that would greatly aid our enemies rather than help our troops and those of our allies that were left there to continue the fight. *Once again, we have to ask ourselves why...*

We also have to ask why Obama completely evacuated Iraq after a war had been fought there: and won; and left that country in jeopardy of being taken over by radicals, which indeed, it almost was. Cities that cost so many lives to free were literally given back to the Islamic extremists. Those same cities now have cost even more lives to re-take and that job is still not done. This evacuation also left Iraq's oil industry as an easy target, which the extremists immediately took over. But, they didn't destroy the oil wells. They need the billions from that oil to finance their operations worldwide. And indeed, it is this oil that has supplied the finances for their terrorist operations.

Add to these things the unrealistic Rules of Engagement that Obama has imposed on our own soldiers: rules, which serve the enemy. Like forbidding the destruction of columns of trucks delivering fuel to our enemies for their military vehicles because the drivers of the trucks might be civilians. These drivers know very well whom they are delivering the fuel to. Rules like these are preposterous and our military leaders have been very much opposed to them. This one restriction has allowed the enemy free movement throughout the region. It is but one restriction: there are many more.

Perhaps the best measure of Barack Obama's feeble war on terror is the amount of deaths from Islamic terrorism during his term. According to retired General Jack Keane, in 2010 there were 3,000 deaths at the hands of Islamic terrorists worldwide; in 2015, the terrorists killed more than 28,000.

There is also a regional genocide being exacted against Christians in the Mid-East by ISIS in which Christians (including women and children) are being beheaded, crucified and literally burned alive. Neither Barack Obama nor Hillary Clinton has done much about this. Rarely is it even mentioned by either of them.

Many of these people are Syrian Christians who are in grave danger and truly in need of being granted refugee status and evacuated from the region. But… of the ten thousand Syrian refugees brought here by Barack Obama **less than one half of one percent of them are Christians!**

Ask yourself why…

****

As for the rest of the foreign policy of the Obama /Hillary team: it has been an unmitigated disaster everywhere. It has been failure after failure including the highly touted "Reset with Russia." Immediately after Hillary's *superb negotiations* Russia began military expansionism: invading territories and even countries.

China has begun expansionism in the Pacific, threatening Taiwan and so on. The failures are everywhere. The truth is that neither Barack Obama nor Hillary Clinton has even one foreign policy success that they can point to. Their efforts have absolutely made the world much more dangerous today than when they assumed power. And... by a long shot!

Gross Negligence

Imagine that you wake up early one morning and go to turn on a light and it doesn't work. You try another light. It doesn't work. Soon you find out that none of your lights work. So you grab your cell phone to call the electric company, but that phone doesn't work either. Now you're starting to panic. What in the hell is going on, you think to yourself.

Finally you grab a flashlight and manage to get to your car in the garage. To your shock: the car doesn't start either. It doesn't even turn over. At this point you realize that something serious has happened so you run outside to go to your neighbor's house and when you do you see that everyone in the neighborhood is already out on the street with flashlights on, too.

In the distance you can see the silhouette of an airliner falling to the earth: followed by an explosion. Then there are screams from your neighbors: they saw it too.

In minutes all of you are realizing that there is no power anywhere. People in the crowd of neighbors are beginning to panic now. Then another of your neighbors comes riding up on a bike. He tells all of you that's he's just been to the bank on the corner. Guess what? The ATM's not working. Soon all of you have the numbing realization that your town is blacked out. And it's then that you realize that... it's not just your town. It's every town.

Finally someone comes out of a house with a survival radio, which is blaring out the news that a state of emergency has been declared and that your city and many others in The United States have been hit by an electro magnetic pulse (EMP) attack from parties unknown. The announcer on the radio continues to report that planes are falling out of the skies and the entire power grid is starting to go down. The government is not functioning and is unable to help at all. Then you hear that it will be several months before any recovery to the power systems can be expected.

You all look at each other, numb with the knowledge that you will all have to fend for yourselves for six months or even longer. The realization that there will be lawless mobs, lootings, murders, rapes, famine, disease and worse ahead of you starts to sink in. The entire society has been shut down and all of you are now forced to be survivalists. You're on your own. You begin eyeing each other suspiciously.

Is this science fiction or a doomsday movie? NO. It is a scenario for which we are all at risk and that is absolutely plausible. In such a scenario, with our current state of preparedness you could expect that it would be three months before you could expect any help and six months before even limited power would be restored and: Total power might never be restored! How's that for an existential risk, Mr. President? And Mr. Biden?

Recently, Joe Biden gave an address wherein he stated that terrorism ***doesn't*** *pose an existential threat to The United States. Really...?*

Over the past eight years Barack Obama and the federal government have done next to nothing to protect us against this threat. They certainly could have (they have known about this for years) and furthermore they should have. But did they? No.

According to Dr. Peter Pry, the Executive Director of the Task Force on National Homeland Security for the Congress of The United States it would take a mere 2 billion dollars to protect the essential elements of our power grid. He further specifies that only twenty billion dollars would protect the entire power grid from an EMP attack. But he warns that if nothing is done, the U.S. might NEVER recover from a large EMP attack.

So why haven't they done anything? Barrack Obama and the politicians would probably tell you that they don't have the money. They certainly have not made this critical issue a priority. An issue that would affect every single American: man, woman and child and literally destroy our entire society.

Bear in mind that, in the last seven years Barack Obama has spent more than TWENTY- TRILLION DOLLARS on his agenda.

That's a thousand, billion dollars - times twenty! So, obviously it's not the money. Twenty billion dollars is a spit in the ocean compared to what these politicians waste every year, let alone the total of what they spend.

Also keep in mind that twenty billion dollars is what we give away in foreign aid to just one country (Pakistan) every year. Ask yourself this: Wouldn't that money have been better spent on upgrading our grid to protect us from this type of disaster? *Yes, ask yourself...*

In fact, our president and all of our politicians are guilty of gross and almost criminal negligence by not doing anything except upgrading the military's grid. That's right, the military grid. The rest of us are on our own. Nothing is being done to address this VERY REAL RISK while billions are paid out for illegal aliens and Syrian refugees.

****

FIVE

Transparency, Scandals, Corruption and... Treachery

Quite contrary to Barack Obama's repeated assertions that his is the most transparent administration in history; it has actually has proven itself to be the least transparent and the most flagrantly lawless, abusive and corrupt presidency in the recent history of The United States and *perhaps all of U.S. history.*

But what's worse is that even after the illegal activities of Barack Obama's administration are uncovered and made public... there are never any CONSEQUENCES. No consequences whatsoever!

It is a matter of public record that Barack Obama, his agents and minions have been allowed to break law after law, target, discriminate against and impose punitive actions upon innocent people or political adversaries: and NOTHING ever happens!

There is, however, one common denominator amongst all of the people that are perpetrating these illegal travesties: **they are all Democrats.**

For the sake of brevity I have highlighted just a few of these travesties and abuses of power. Let's start with the most recent.

Hillary Clinton's Email Investigation

Attorney General Loretta Lynch and the Department of Justice have recently announced that the balance of Hillary Clinton's illegal emails (those that are top government level and those that deal with the Clinton Foundation) will not be released for more than twenty-two months! That will, of course, be well after this presidential election is over.

It will also, of course, deprive the American people of the knowledge of the truth about the potentially illegal activities of Barack Obama's highest ranking administration official while she held office.

Two days after this announcement Loretta Lynch had a private and secret meeting with Bill Clinton at an airport in Phoenix, Arizona. Not only was this unethical and a clear conflict of interest with any honest investigation, but it was also against the regulations of The Department of Justice, which Loretta Lynch is in charge of! Bill Clinton could very well have been a defendant in the investigation of Hillary using her position as Secretary of State to trade influence for cash to the Clinton Foundation. So, even the appearance of propriety was thrown out the window.

Loretta Lynch then offered up the feeble and insulting statement that she would make her decisions on this case based upon the recommendations of the FBI and the career attorneys at the DOJ. Really...? At the very least this woman should have removed herself from any involvement with this case.

Aside form the obvious conflicts of interest there was also the fact that it was Bill Clinton, himself, who had appointed Loretta Lynch to her high profile position as U.S. Attorney for the eastern district of New York. It is not at all likely that she would ever have risen to the United States Attorney General's position had it not been for that high profile appointment.

Quid pro quo...? Ask yourself...

Now, Attorney General Loretta Lynch has refused to take any investigation of the Clinton Foundation and bribery allegations against Hillary Clinton by the FBI seriously. Simply put: Loretta Lynch will not bring any charges against Clinton; even if there is a criminal referral by the FBI.

Another quid pro quo, or cover up? Ask yourself...

If Hillary Clinton were a Republican the same biased, dishonest liberal press that has minimized all of this would have been screaming at the top of their lungs for her prosecution; and they would be right to do so.

Loretta Lynch should resign and if Barack Obama were an honest man (which, clearly, he is not) he would demand her resignation.

The mainstream media has, of course, made light of these incidents and moreover, has not given any credence to the assertions by legal authorities that Hillary Clinton's use of a private email server was a clear violation of federal law (U.S. Code 18 among others) that imposed high level security risks for The United States as well as for the people working undercover overseas in the intelligence services: because names were listed in those emails.

Indeed, one man has already been executed in Iran after his name appeared in some of Hillary's emails. Was it the emails that revealed him? We don't know, but this is an actual example of how Hillary Clinton cavalierly puts peoples' lives in danger for the sake of her personal ambitions and ill-gotten gains.

And now, virtually every week, more of Hillary's nefarious and very illegal activities as Secretary of State are being found out about in more and more of these notorious emails of hers, wherein she traded her influence and gave favors as the Secretary of State in return for huge sums of money that were given to her Clinton Foundation. These huge sums now add up to almost 2 billion dollars.

Even now Bill and Hillary Clinton refuse to stop taking money from foreign interests for their foundation, unless, of course, she should be elected as the president of The United States.

Really...? Well, if it would be wrong for Hillary Clinton to be involved with this foundation while serving as the president, why then would it have been OK for her to be involved in her foundation as the Secretary of State?

Here is but one example of Hillary's nefarious dealings: Acting as the Secretary of State, Hillary personally made possible the takeover of one of America's largest uranium producing companies (Uranium One) by Russian interests. Of course, Russia could then sell the uranium to Iran, which needs it for their nuclear weapons programs: Being the Secretary of State at the time Hillary Clinton had to approve this deal, which she did.

And uranium was indeed sold to Iran.

After this deal had been consummated it was then reported that the Clinton Foundation pocketed 135 million dollars for Hillary's role in getting the deal through. This is illegal to say the least: but also treacherous and un-patriotic, unless Hillary considers Iran to be an ally of The United States, which it most certainly is not. Their leader still chants "Death to America," publicly and Iran is still the world's largest sponsor of Islamic terrorism.

You're probably asking yourself why an American official in such a high station do such a thing.

Yes, ask yourself, but make sure you follow the money when you do.

There really was no chance of an indictment of Hillary for her lawless behavior because, like all of Obama's appointees, even Attorneys General and FBI directors too, are required to leave their integrity at the door when they take up their positions under Obama. Loretta Lynch is an excellent example of this. Sadly, now even the last of our once great institutions of justice (the FBI) has been sucked down into Barack Obama's cesspool of lies and corruption.

The IRS Scandal

Once again, a high-ranking official of the Obama Administration was caught using her authority to ILLEGALLY harass, persecute, punish and otherwise stifle conservative opponents of Barack Obama and the Democratic Party. And, once again, this was also **done in the run up to Barack Obama's re-election in 2012.** Coincidence? *Ask yourself...*

Lois Lerner (the official in question) not only intimidated legitimate non-profits from operating under their non-profit status, she actually targeted these organizations and the individuals who ran them for prosecution by the Department of Justice and even sent taxpayers' confidential information on the individuals to the DOJ for the purposes of prosecuting them under false and contrived pretenses. This takes **illegality under the color of authority** to new levels. These are reminiscent of the tactics that were used in the old Soviet Union. It's no wonder that this truly evil woman took the fifth when she was called in to testify before Congress. To call this woman "scum" would be to flatter her.

This is yet another example that reveals just how comfortable Democrats are to abuse their authority and break any law and destroy innocent people so long as it serves to advance the political agenda of the Democratic Party.

This is also yet another example of how Barack Obama's Federal Agencies and the officials that run them are illegally using their authority and abusing their corresponding powers to oppress and repress their political opponents.

These tactics are not progressive. They also are not democratic, either. They are however... **fascist and totalitarian.**

There are other notorious scandals in this administration such as the Fast and Furious Gun Scandal, in which the administration gave thousands of assault rifles to Mexican drug cartels (the very guns that the Democrats are trying to outlaw right now). These very guns have been traced to the use of them by these cartels to murder thousands of people in Mexico and numerous others on our side of the border. Because this program involved people at the top (Eric Holder) no one was ever held accountable for this deadly fiasco.

There was also the failure of Eric Holder's DOJ from prosecuting the New Black Panthers for voter intimidation in the 2008 presidential elections, many incidents of which, were actually verified by several videos taken at polling locations.

The Benghazi Cover Up

The attacks at Benghazi, Libya on 9-11 of 2012 have already been covered in this book. However, it is not the deaths and injuries to the Americans there that is scandalous. What those people suffered was tragic.

What was scandalous was what was "not done" to provide the protection that those victims had repeatedly and desperately asked for and the selfish reasons that both Barack Obama and Hillary Clinton had for trying to cover up what truly happened there and then to try and absolve themselves from any responsibility for the incident. This is what was, and still is, scandalous.

These are but a few of the controversial and scandalous actions undertaken by officials of this most lawless administration. But, here are others:

Obama Care

Nancy Pelosi famously said, "We have to pass the bill to see what's in it." And, yes, she did say that with a straight face. *More disdain...*

Barack Obama famously said, "If you like your doctor, you can keep your doctor." He also said, "If you like your insurance company you can keep your insurance company." He knew full well that both of these statements were flagrant lies, whose only purpose was to deceive the American people.

And on it goes… discrimination and abuses of power against conservative citizens of this country are now exercised by virtually every agency of our federal government.

And why? It's because under Barack Obama, nearly all of these agencies are headed by Progressive Democrats (liberals) appointed by him and, all of who, use neither morality, the truth, or even the law itself to guide their actions. Instead it's all about their plan to achieve power and total control over this country. This lawless president has given them all the go ahead, (both tacitly and through his own example) to push the limits.

We now live in a completely lawless country because lawlessness, as does lawfulness, starts at the top. And just as Barack Obama gave legitimacy, and therefore license, to black criminals to continue to commit violent crimes by declaring publicly, along with Eric Holder, that blacks in America are being discriminated against by the criminal justice system and even went so far as to say that they are being targeted and deliberately persecuted (which is a blatant lie that flies in the face of the facts), he has also encouraged members of his party that either hold elective office, or have been appointed by him, to abuse their offices and break the law themselves. They have only to look to him for their example. It's "shoved down your throat" government and the hell with the citizens of this country if they don't like it.

Now, because of the cowardice of the Director of the FBI and the Congress, the citizens of this country are left with not even one agency in this huge and onerous federal government to protect them from the corrupt and lawless persecutions of that most dishonest and corrupt federal government. Save a miracle; we are lost…

*It should be noted here that a primary reason for The Constitution of The United States was to **LIMIT** the size and power of the Federal Government.*

****

SIX

The Two Economies

Yes, that's right: There have been two economies in The United States since 2009; since the moment Barack Obama took office and rescued all the rest of us from a second "Great Depression." At least according to him.

This is the one that; by the claims of Barack Obama and the Democrats, has made a miraculous recovery and now is both strong and stable.

Then, there is the other one: you know, the one that we, and the 94 million out of work Americans have lived with everyday for the last seven and a half years. The one that we all experience every time we go to the grocery store or pay our *higher* health insurance premiums (the premiums that were supposed to be lower because of Obama Care), or wrestle with the 3,000 dollars less of household incomes that we all have now, or try to adjust our household budgets to deal with the non-existent inflation that we are all experiencing: Oh, well… why quibble.

This November the health care costs for the average American family will increase by $4,100 per year!

Talk about being out of touch with reality…

Barrack Obama thinks that because he says something it is automatically accepted as reality. His claims belie the truth, which is that we have never had a real economic recovery. In fact, he has the distinction of being the only president who has never had at least one year of 3% growth in the economy, which is considered to be modest. Over his eight years in office the United States economy has achieved a paltry 2% of GDP (growth). This happens to be, by the way, the lowest GDP growth on record! This year GDP growth has dropped to a pitiful 1%.

And, those low unemployment figures are false too, in the sense that they don't include those 94 million Americans who have given up and dropped out of the system. Add to that the fact that the majority of the jobs "created" by Obama are of a menial nature and either part time positions or for 30 hours a week or less (due to Obama Care mandates to employers); leaving those millions of employees with not only lower incomes, but also higher health care costs that they have to pay on their own! Health care costs have risen by two and three times for Americans since the institution of Obama's, so called, Affordable Health Care Act and they are about to go up again: by a lot!

Of course, Barack Obama doesn't want to go near the unemployment figures for black Americans of well over 20% on the whole and a staggering 59% for black teenage males. If Obama were to comment on these issues I'm sure he'd chalk it up to racism again, but in the case of the black male teenager it has nothing to do with racism. What it does have to do with are the school dropout rates in this population group: leaving these kids with few skills to bring to the table when applying for a job.

These kids leaving school early are illiterate with terrible grammar and no skills, making them less than desirable for hire even at low level customer service or retail clerk level. Whose fault it is that these kids are dropping out of school is another issue. Frankly, it is an issue that Barack Obama should be talking about: and addressing continually. But he won't: doesn't fit his white Americans are racist narrative.

He's also doubled the national debt by running it up to 20 TRILLION DOLLARS, which is unsustainable. This approaches the total Gross Domestic Productivity number for The United States. Why is this so important? Because it is the tipping point that will cause the boat to sink. That boat being the United States of America. Do you think it possible that Barack Obama doesn't know this? *Ask yourself...*

By the way: this too, is part of the Socialists' strategy for toppling a capitalistic society: make its debt so huge that it becomes untenable; thereby enabling a Socialist government to take over.

Obama continually points out that he had to rescue us and right the ship after George Bush's economic disaster in 2008. Really... what he doesn't say is that it was the Bill Clinton and the Democratic Party that caused the U.S. economy to meltdown in the first place. Clinton's National Partnership In Home Ownership policy forced lending institutions to lend money to people who had no credit history and simply could not afford to pay a mortgage.

This policy was specifically directed at minorities and, in particular, African Americans. Why? Probably the usual reason: to get their votes.

Remember Clinton's braggadocio about being the first black president and all that.

Under this policy banks and lenders were intimidated by the Clinton Justice Department if they didn't bend the rules and make extremely high risk loans to minorities: which created the crisis, which by the way, George Bush had warned us about. His warning, of course, fell on deaf ears and Democrats (like Barney Frank) sharply told him to back off and leave the policy alone and... that it was in no danger of collapsing.

The economic disaster that followed was the direct result of Bill Clinton's policies. The homeowners didn't pay the banks back, the banks started failing, then Wall Street and so on. The ripple effect was devastating to all but rich Americans. So, once again, it was the Democratic Party that caused the problem in the first place *to get their minority votes.* They then spent years (with the help of the dishonest, biased press) lying about it and shifting the blame on George Bush, who had nothing to do with it. Bill Clinton and the Democratic Party were responsible for the housing bubble and the crash of the economy.

Under Barack Obama home ownership has fallen to the lowest level it has been at for over FIFTY YEARS!

You will never hear the truth out of the mouth of Barack Obama about this. Instead, he points out that he saved GM and the U.S. auto industry and that now the American car industry is booming with record sales. Yes, record sales: just like the record housing sales before the 2008 housing crash. The same things are happening with cars that happened with houses. Car loans are being given to people who can't afford to pay them back (and probably won't) and a new bubble is being created in the auto credit industry just as it was in the housing industry. So, in fact, Obama really doesn't even have one section of the economy that he or his policies have positively affected. Not even one...

Finally, Obama's targeting of the coal industry has led to massive layoffs, unemployment and deprivation for hundreds of thousands of formerly working Americans and their families, throwing these people into poverty. Does he care? *Ask yourself...* Worse yet, Hillary Clinton is bragging about how she's going to put tens of thousands more of these people out of work.

So why are Obama and Hillary targeting the coal industry when really there isn't any reason to do this? Answer: They need the money and votes from the environmentalists, that's why. So, it's the hell with the economy and the hell with the families supported by good-paying jobs in this industry.

The coal industry has been the backbone of our energy industry (it still provides most of our electricity) and the American coal mining companies have made massive strides in cleaning up that industry. Their "clean coal" mining programs have worked marvelously. Today there is absolutely NO REASON to shut down the coal industry. Maybe 30 years ago: but not now. But, to Barack Obama and Hillary Clinton it's all about politics. Oh, and money of course...

There is one other reason that the Democrats and Obama are targeting the energy industry though: CONTROL. They have to have total control over the society. So, just as they made the power grab over health care, they are also doing it with energy.

After all, for a totalitarian socialist state to succeed, it has to control all the major industries in the economy. Otherwise the totalitarian part won't work.

*Hillary Clinton was the first person that wanted to force a national single payer healthcare system on Americans. And... **she wanted to send people to jail if they didn't sign up.** Remember... It's totalitarianism that they want.*

The whole global warning/climate change scare is really about control as well. NASA satellites have accurately recorded that there has been NO INCREASE to the earth's temperature for twenty-two years. None.

The government and university scientists on the other hand have been using computer models, which are obviously NOT ACCURATE to forecast global warming. And keep in mind that most of the scientists are getting grants for their studies so their findings are definitely influenced by the government's agenda. If they don't go along with the government's agenda they lose their grants (which is their source of income).

Follow the money: It's about control...

****

SEVEN

The Vast LEFT WING (Media) Conspiracy

For more than twenty years Hillary Clinton has been peddling the idea that there is a "Vast Right Wing Conspiracy" that was out to get both her and her husband Bill. She has repeatedly attempted to use this farcical conspiracy to deflect attention from Bill's lascivious misdeeds as well as her own shady and nefarious activities. But what is the truth? Is there really a vast right wing media conspiracy?

Well, let's see... was it the right wing media that minimized (when they bothered to report on it at all) the seriousness of Hillary's use of a private email server instead of legally required, secure government servers?

Was it the vast right wing media conspiracy that minimized the threats to national security by Hillary for this nefarious (and very illegal) practice?

Was it the vast right wing media conspiracy that overlooked the tens of millions of dollars Hillary (ostensibly for the Clinton Foundation) took in from foreign governments; many of which are not allies of The United States WHILE SHE WAS SECRETARY OF STATE?

Many of these contributing countries were Arabian Muslim countries that still practice Sharia law, which victimizes women, gays, Christians, Jews and anyone that does not convert to Islam.

Was it the vast right wing conspiracy that spread the lie about the reason for the Benghazi attacks on 911 of 2012 and then deliberately failed to mention that Hillary's interventionist follies in Libya were what was actually the reason for the attacks?

Was it the vast right wing conspiracy that wouldn't give voice to the survivors of the Benghazi attacks who had publicly testified that help was held back during the 13 hours of those attacks? Or that Hillary Clinton had not responded to more than 600 requests for help in the months leading up to those attacks from the people that she herself had sent to that station?

Was it the vast right wing media conspiracy that was responsible for hiding the facts and NOT REPORTING on the real and infamous background of the very much anti-American, radical presidential candidate Barack Obama in both 2008 and 2012?

And, was it the vast right wing conspiracy that provided cover for the IRS's illegal and abusive scandals, gave validity to the outright lie of "Hands Up, Don't Shoot" in Ferguson, Missouri, hid the deceits concerning Obama-Care, Fast and Furious, the Iran Nuclear Deal and on and on and on?

Was it the vast right wing conspiracy that has failed to report on Hillary's involvement in, and responsibility for, the treacherous sale and transfer of uranium assets first to Russia and, in turn, then to Iran?

No, of course it wasn't because there is no vast right wing conspiracy and there never has been. There is, however, a vast left wing conspiracy that has deliberately given favoritism to, and covered for, Democrats while spreading outright lies about conservatives and this has been going on since long before Hillary and Bill Clinton were in the Whitehouse. This conspiracy involves the traditional press, the media and TV, and the majority of the country's high school and college teachers, who have even gone so far as to revise the actual history of The United States to show the country in a bad light. It is, indeed, decades old by now.

Over 94% of all of the journalists in The United States are self-avowed liberal Democrats, or in modern parlance: Progressives. These people have both individually, and collectively, thrown their ethics out the window and misreported the nation's news with overwhelming favoritism extended to the left and Democrats whilst routinely doing hatchet jobs on any Republicans and especially conservative Republicans. More often than not their reporting borders on lies and most certainly does routinely omit any negative reporting about Democratic politicians; especially Barack Obama and now, of course, Hillary Clinton.

As has already been stated: lies of omission are still lies...

This blind allegiance to "The Party" has gotten so bad now that these media personalities and TV networks don't even bother to hide their obvious bias, editorialize everything in favor of their party and, even worse, completely ignore their responsibility and that of their agencies to report the truth to the American public.

And, it is very sad to have to say that this is very reminiscent of the press and media of the old communist Soviet Union.

The American media has now gone far past partisan reporting of the news. Now they are actually engaging in engineering elections in this country for the Democratic Party and its candidates.

This is an absolute betrayal of the American people and it is a betrayal of the highest order. Freedom of the press in given to news organizations precisely so that they have the ability to report the "truth" without fear of prosecution or recriminations for that reporting.

****

EIGHT

The Real Legacy of Barack Hussein Obama

When Barry Soetoro took on the name Barack Hussein Obama he also assumed a persona that is in keeping with his current policies concerning the United States and Islam, in particular. This book is testimony to that.

There has been much said on social media sites about the fact that he applied for and received a fellowship from the Fullbright Foundation for foreign students by applying as an Indonesian citizen. More recently, there is much being said about the claim that his *actual* birth certificate has surfaced, allegedly proving that he was born in Kenya and not the United States: thereby making him ineligible to hold the office of President of the United States. An allegation that is supported (critics say) by a statement Michelle Obama supposedly made on an African trip where, when in Kenya, she stated that she was happy to be in the country of her husband's birth.

These things and the questions relating to his actual parentage, his having flunked out of Occidental College, how he really got accepted into Harvard and got a staff position there due to an alleged Saudi Arabian cash donation to the prestigious University as well as the allegation that Mr. Barry Soetoro never attended Columbia University at all, his ties to Bill Ayres (an admitted terrorist) and his relationship with Jeremiah Wright all have been given no credence and swept under the rug by the Democratic Party and the biased, liberal, Democratic TV networks and press. At the very least, they should have been honestly investigated and the truth reported to the American people.

Suffice it to say that there is little that can be done about it now: the damage has been done. And boy, what damage… We have never seen damage like this by any president in this nation's history. He makes the worst of them look like saints.

The problem is that the damage Barack Obama has deliberately done to this country will affect all of us for a long time. The damage is so massive that a new president, even with eight years in office, won't be able to correct it all. Add to that fact that the Democratic Party and the complicit media will make it as difficult as possible to undo Obama's many destructive policies and Obama will have the federal courts on his side long after he has left office.

Barack Obama has appointed 329 liberal judges to the federal bench since he's been president. Through these appointments he has managed to change the thirteen, once conservative and centrist federal courts, to very far left leaning courts in nine of those thirteen federal districts. These are the courts to which cases are brought before they get to the Supreme Court. And, by the way, these judgeships are lifetime appointments...

Like I said: Long after he's left office...

The real legacy of Barack Hussein Obama will be the degradations to our culture and society and the demise of this once great country that he has personally and deliberately caused.

But the very same partisan, biased press and media that lied to the people to get him elected and that have protected him for the last eight years (*when they knew of his background and notorious past*) will be the very institutions that will write the legacy of this very, very wicked and un-American man.

Then the academics and historians will use these same falsehoods that were propagated by Barack Obama himself, the Democratic Party and that biased, dishonest liberal media to deceive Americans and get this man elected in the first place. From this phony provenance and contrived history the historians will write Barack Hussein Obama's fake and fraudulent biography.

Sadly, it will be a long time before Americans learn about the real history and spurious background of this charlatan. A spurious background filled with falsehoods and lies. And when Americans do learn the truth about Barack Hussein Obama they will be, at first shocked, but then outraged that the liberal left and their favorite TV news personalities lied and omitted the truth about this man to pull off this greatest and most costly fraud ever put over on the American people. A fraud filled with treachery directed at the United States of America for the purposes of dismantling our constitutional and capitalistic system and transforming this country into a totalitarian, socialist state.

So, what is the real legacy of Barack Obama?

Tragically, it is one of treachery and betrayal. Devious treachery towards the American people and then the betrayal of the country that provided him with the unique opportunity to drag himself up and out of obscurity and then gave him the fantastic opportunity to rise to the most prominent political position in the world.

What was Barack Obama's repayment to the American people for this honor? A constant stream of lies, deceptions and cons all leading up to the many fraudulent acts that he has perpetrated upon us. His real legacy is truly… one of betrayal and moral turpitude.

****

NINE

The Democratic Party Going Forward

In 1787 Benjamin Franklin had just left Independence Hall in Philadelphia after signing the newly created Constitution of The United States.

As he walked down the street a woman approached him and asked, "So which did you give us Dr. Franklin, a monarchy, or a republic?"

"A republic, madam," he said to her, "If you can keep it,".

Franklin's sardonic caveat to that woman is more important today than it was even on that day in 1787. And the reason why is The Democratic Party.

Since the beginning of the twentieth century (early in the 1900's) this party has been trying to usurp our Constitution and turn The United States into a socialist country. As Marxism was growing in Europe at that time: so it was here.

The Declaration of Independence was written to declare our freedom from England's monarch or that of any other country. And, it was also to declare the freedoms given to us by God; and declare that those freedoms supersede any of those given by man.

It is important to remember that the word "ourselves" in the preamble of the United States Constitution was a word of great significance to the founders of this country. Their intention was that the majority of regulatory powers for the governance of the country were to be left to (the people of) the individual states and *not* vested in a federal, national government.

As we have all seen in the last seven years, the Barack Obama presidency has made the federal government bigger and more intrusive and controlling than it has ever been.

And, as evidenced by the rise and popularity of Bernie Sanders in 2016, the Democratic Party has indoctrinated the youth of this country to the point that socialism has become more appealing than our constitutional republic and the capitalistic system that made this country great and produced better standards of living for its people than any society in history.

The aforementioned indoctrination has been accomplished through liberal (Democratic) control of the vast majority of our media (especially the mainstream TV networks) and virtually all of our educational institutions: including grammar schools, high schools and colleges.

These academic institutions have engaged in "revisionist history" and lies deliberately designed to diminish the actual role of The United States in the world's history from the American Revolution, to anti-slavery abolitionism, to the Civil War, and even to World War II, which, had The United States not won it, would have had us all living under complete totalitarianism or Nazism to this day.

****

So, what will the Democratic Party do going forward?

Voter Fraud

It will most certainly do more of *all of the above,* but first thing's first. The Democratic Party will again engage in widespread voter fraud. They always do…

But, there will be *unbridled* voter fraud by the Democratic Party in this year's elections. And it will be worse than it has been before. After what the Democrats have accomplished in the last eight years under Barack Obama don't think for a minute that there is anything that they won't do to keep their power. There was plenty of voter fraud in the last two presidential elections, but there will be much more in the 2016 elections because the Obama administration has shown that it will not enforce any laws that impede his agenda. And that agenda calls for more socialism and division.

AND, the Progressive, liberal Democrats are also using federal courts to advance voter fraud and illegally influence elections. Just recently North Carolina's Voter I.D. state law was ruled as being discriminatory towards minorities by a liberal court. Don't think this to be an isolated incident. Any voter I.D. initiatives, no matter where, are constantly challenged by the

Democrats, and always on the basis of discrimination: usually referring to blacks and Hispanics.

Their (the Democrats) contention is that it is a HARDSHIP for minorities and especially blacks to obtain legal ID's and therefore many black voters will be deprived of their right to vote. You have to ask yourself: Just how disdainful of blacks and other minorities are the liberals?

Yes, ask yourself...

No, of course this nonsensical excuse is not the real reason for blocking voter ID laws. If it was, then blacks and other minority groups wouldn't be required to have Driver's licenses to drive, or ID's to cash checks, get credit cards, buy cars, get on planes, etc. Blacks and other minorities seem to have NO PROBLEM obtaining ID's for all these things.

Add to this that legal state ID's can be obtained at any DMV office, by mail or even online. So, then, what is the real reason that the Democrats don't want people to have to show identification to vote? *Ask yourself...*

There have been numerous reports of people voting more than once in locations where legal identification wasn't required: sometimes at the very same locations!

There have also been numerous instances where people have voted for candidates that were dead. The candidates weren't dead: but the people casting the votes were, though. Funny that they're always Democratic voters...

No, this is clearly an effort by the liberals and Democrats to illegally sway election results in their favor. They have had the ability to commit large-scale voter fraud for a long time (as ACORN did in 2008) and now any effort to take that ploy away will be fiercely challenged; legally through the courts and otherwise. And the practices will continue.

A Liberal, Socialist, Politically Correct Supreme Court

It was the Supreme Court that forced Obama Care on the nation, which so crippled our country economically and it was the Supreme Court that forced gay marriage on our culture and *it will be* the Supreme Court that will take away Second Amendment gun rights, stand your ground laws, States voter ID laws and on and on.

This will be so if a Democrat should win the Whitehouse because it is part of the Progressive, liberal, Democratic Party strategy to undo The United States Constitution and the constitutional rights of U.S. citizens by using the courts to achieve these results.

Up to now the Democrats have repeatedly tested our Constitution, but should a Democratic Party candidate be elected to the presidency they will own the Supreme Court and use it to strip conservatives of their rights and undo many of the original amendments that have to do with religious freedom, the right to bear arms and even freedom of speech.

America will then become a socialist, very much fascist and totalitarian country in short order.

An Even Weaker and Tepid Economy

Hillary Clinton has basically rubber stamped the economic strategies of Barack Obama and fully intends to continue with them. She has no new ideas except to tax the rich. But, she has deliberately NOT ruled out tax increases for everyone but the very poorest of us.

Unfortunately, even this will not begin to pay for all of the things she is promising to provide for free, such as: college tuition, government paid abortions and much, much more. Why is she promising all of these for free?

Ask yourself...

She is not going to reduce any of the thousands of federal regulations that are strangling small businesses in this country, nor is Hillary going to undo any of the thousands of new debilitating regulations enacted by the Obama Administration. Instead, to please the environmentalists, she will strangle American industries like the coal industry and small businesses (the real engine of the U.S. economy) even further by adding untold numbers of new regulations to please the left and the environmentalists.

It has gotten harder for Americans to start small businesses with each passing day of the Obama Administration. Should Hillary Clinton be elected... it will get harder yet.

Even Larger Intrusive Federal Government and Higher taxes

Think about what this huge federal monstrosity has brought us? It is responsible for now millions of incompetent government employees that abuse their offices and fail at the simplest responsibilities of their jobs.

On top of this widespread incompetence, small businesses across America have made increasing numbers of complaints about unrealistic and costly regulations being enforced by nameless and un-elected bureaucrats in all of these government agencies. Regulations enacted by these agencies become (de facto) federal laws and carry with them civil, financial and even criminal punishments for non-compliance. Thousands of regulations are enacted into law every year and no one puts a stop to it or even tries to reign in these agencies or the pompous and partisan autocrats that run them.

Congress has been either blind or spineless in stopping this abuse of power. They have literally done nothing and left individual Americans to fight for themselves in the courts. In all too many instances these people are put out of business or even fined and jailed. This truly is TYRANNY.

Our Constitution specifies that only the Congress of The United States can enact federal laws, yet these agencies reign over us strangling businesses and even landowners' use of their own property.

Open Immigration and the Elimination of U.S. Borders

Obama has already ignored federal law and defied federal court rulings against his actions. He's opened the borders, ordered the Border Patrol and Customs agents to stand back and let the illegal immigrants flood into the country and has used every method at his disposal to bring more than a million Muslims into the country as well, with no regard to safety or security threats posed by diseases or the financial burdens these immigrants pose to the American people.

Hillary Clinton has declared publicly that she will not only continue Barack Obama's policies, but that she will expand them; many times over. And as already mentioned in this book it has been reported that she intends to eliminate America's borders altogether, which will bring immigrants here from Central and South America as well as more Mexicans in the tens of millions!

These millions would then be registered as Democratic voters, thereby ensuring complete domination in American politics by the Democratic Party. This of course, will accomplish the Democratic Party's goal to have overwhelming voter superiority for all elections.

Massive Immigration of Un-vetted Islamic Refugees

For years now Barack Obama has bent rules or just ignored the law to bring as many Muslims as possible into the United States. Tashfeen Malik: the woman terrorist and murderer at San Bernardino last December is but one example of how he has bent the rules.

Now Hillary Clinton wants to increase the number of Syrian refugees that Obama had planned to bring into the U.S. by more than 500 percent! And yes, she knows that these refugees cannot be vetted and pose a great danger to the citizens of The United States.

Let us all remember that all of the heads of the federal agencies that provide the nation's security have publicly stated and warned us that these refugees cannot be vetted, their backgrounds cannot be checked and that this influx of refugees will almost certainly be infiltrated by ISIS, if not other terrorist groups as well.

More Racial Strife

The Democratic Party is responsible for the racial strife in this country. It is the Democrats who are responsible for the inner city ghettos, the welfare culture and the decline of education in The United States. The Democrats run most city governments in this country and have for the last 50 years. The Democrats have also had control of the education system in this country for the past fifty years. It was the Democratic Party that created the welfare state with blacks in mind. Lyndon Johnson has been quoted as having said at the time, "If we give them niggers welfare we'll have their votes for 200 years." It was not a Republican saying that; it was a Democratic President.

It was also the Democratic Party that fought FOR SLAVERY. It was the Democratic Party that started the Ku Klux Klan in the old Democratic Party controlled south. It was the Democratic Party that enacted the Jim Crowe laws in the south after they (The Confederacy) lost the Civil War. It was also the Democratic Party that fought against the Civil Rights Act in the 1960's and, in fact, President Lyndon Johnson had to get the Republicans in Congress at that time to give him the votes to pass his Civil Rights Act, which struck down the Jim Crowe laws and ended legal segregation in the south.

You, of course, won't learn this from any modern history books in our schools today because the Democratic Party (through their control of the education system and teacher's unions) has replaced the true history with revisionist history that casts all of America as being racist, which it certainly was not. Most of the northern states were against slavery and had been since the founding of this country. And, the Republican Party had been against slavery from its founding.

The first Republican president was Abraham Lincoln who was very much against slavery and, in fact, the Confederacy was formed and the Civil War started by the southern Democrats *because* Lincoln was elected president in 1860. That indeed, was what provoked the southern states to secede from the Union and to start hostilities at Fort Sumter. Thus began the Civil War.

It is a fact that the Democratic Party had been pro-slavery since its' founding in 1824.Yet the liberals and Democrats have the unmitigated gall to accuse Republicans and conservatives of being racist. And of course, the dishonest media goes right along with them and propagates these lies.

And now it is once again the Democrats causing racial strife and inciting violence and crime across the country led by none other than Barack Obama himself. Hillary Clinton is only going to add to this problem.

The Democratic Party has always promoted discontent and unrest in the black communities of this country and has also always blamed Republicans for the plight of blacks in the inner cities. They've always used conditions among the black population as a wedge issue to divide the country racially and get the black vote. Yet it has been the Democratic Party with largely black administrators that have run these cities and their schools almost entirely. This too, has been true for nearly fifty years now.

With Barack Obama, Hillary Clinton and the Democratic Party all having endorsed Black Lives Matter there is little likelihood that race relations will go back to where they were any time soon. It will get worse before it gets better to be sure. Adding to the problems: the mainstream media and the TV networks are in lockstep with the Democrats; blaming white conservatives for the condition of black society and the police for the death of young black men in America even though this is at odds with the truth. But the truth will not be told by any but a few in the media and the constant drumbeat of these falsities will keep black resentment at explosive levels.

Finally, women's rights advocates should be made aware that it was also the Democratic Party that FOUGHT AGAINST women's right to vote in the early 1900's. The Republicans were for it.

Escalating Crime Rates

Crime is rising at alarming levels, particularly crimes committed by blacks and illegal aliens and nothing is being done about it because we have a president who won't acknowledge the truth about the issue. It was reported by cable news recently that the Obama Administration has even been lying about the amount of crimes committed by illegal aliens in this country and, despite their own statistics, Obama and his Department of Justice won't address the issue of black crime.

Plus, Obama and other Democratic officials are aggressively and unfairly judging police as guilty right off the bat in any shootings or deaths where a black is involved without any regard to the facts in these incidents. This will quite naturally result in police being battle shy if not outright recalcitrant when dealing with African-American suspects. And since the majority of violent offenders are black the result will be even higher crime and it will not be restricted to just black communities. It will spread just as it did in the 1980's and 90's.

More Sanctuary Cities

It needs to be noted that almost all, if not all, of the sanctuary cities in The United States are governed and administrated by Democrats. These cities are havens for illegal aliens who hide out in them safe from apprehension after committing crimes no matter how heinous. The Obama Administration has refused to cut off funding to these cities or address this problem in any way. The result of this has been an increase in the number of illegal criminals coming to America and running free.

These criminals commit crimes all over the country not just in the sanctuary cities, but they flee back to them after committing their crimes. And no one can touch them. This is insane.

It should also be noted that Hillary Clinton has no plans to crack down on these sanctuary cities or address this problem in any way. It might offend Hispanic voters...

Increased Political Correctness

It was the Democrats who invented political correctness. It was invented as a way to control people by using it as a weapon to intimidate them. It is also a tool to stifle and prohibit freedom of speech. *Absolutely necessary for a totalitarian, socialist dystopia...*

If the Democrats are put back in power with the election of a Democratic president we will see political correctness on steroids. It will be given teeth with laws against offensive speech or behavior towards minorities and the Democratic Party's protected classes: blacks, Hispanics, LGBT's and yes Muslims. Excessive protectionist policies will be put in place that will carry criminal punishments for all offenders, who of course will be: white Americans. *Which is exactly the point they wish to make.*

A Continuation of the Failed Educational System

Common Core is the Democrats choice as the new program of educating the nation's kids. But, aside from making simple mathematics very confusing and needlessly harder, most Americans don't know what else Common Core teaches, or more importantly, doesn't teach. This is especially important with regard to history.

In the Common Core program students are NOT taught about the reasons for World War II: At least not the REAL reasons. They are also not taught about Adolf Hitler and the invasion of Europe by Nazi Germany, the invasions of China and the countries throughout the Pacific by Japan or the invasions of North Africa by Italy. Nor are they taught about the barbaric practices or the atrocities and genocides committed by Germany, Japan or Italy in all of their conquests. They are also NOT taught that it was America that had to respond to these invasions and literally save the world from being over run and ruled by these brutal fascist countries: sacrificing 600 thousand Americans dead and millions more maimed for life in the effort.

So what are these students taught? They are taught that The United States UNJUSTLY and wantonly dropped nuclear weapons on cities in Japan without explaining the reasons for this drastic measure at all. They are not taught that Japan refused to surrender after four years of war, leaving The United States with only two options to bring the war to an end. The first option was to invade Japan and the second was to use the Atom Bomb to bring the war to a quick end.

In World War II all of the United States admirals and generals who had been fighting Japan for years advised President Truman that an invasion of the Japanese home islands would cost at least a million American casualties with hundreds of thousands of those troops being killed and would cost the loss of up to five million Japanese lives in the process as well. For President Truman there was no decision other than to drop the bomb and bring an end to the war.

Students today do not realize that there were 70 million people killed in that war with most of those deaths caused by Nazi Germany and Imperial Japan.

So, why would this false REVISIONIST HISTORY be taught to our kids? Once again the answer is to undermine America and show our country in a bad light. Keep in mind that it is, and has been, the Democratic Party that has controlled the educational curriculum in this country. Realizing that: ask yourself the question again.

Remember... It's socialistic totalitarianism that they want.

****

TEN

Hillary's Real History

Hillary Clinton is portraying herself as an advocate for women, children and middle class working people. However, her history shows that she has never fought for these groups, even when she has been in the position to do so.

Instead her real history has been, that since graduating from college, she has lived an extremely privileged life. A life filled with servants and assistants to do her bidding: even insofar as the raising of her daughter. This picture is quite contrary to what Bill Clinton said about Hillary in his speech at the recent Democratic National Convention. His description of Hillary's history is a pure myth: a fantasy of lies, as too was Chelsea Clinton's description of her mother.

Hillary was at every soccer game? Hillary, the soccer Mom? Please...

****

Dick Morris was Hillary Clinton's chief advisor from 1977 through 1997 and communicated with her continually throughout those years. According to Morris, Bill's rendition of Hillary's life is quite at odds with the truth. In his new book, "Armageddon: How Trump Can Beat Hillary" Morris outlines the real history of Hillary Clinton: a history rife with, corruption, Marxist affiliations, swindles and shady business deals, anti-American activities, and of course, privilege. *Always privilege...*

The following are just a few of the sordid incidents in the life of Hillary that Dick Morris has made public now.

Bill Clinton said in his speech that while at law school at Yale in the early 1970's Hillary left the University to spend a year working on the Children's Defense Fund. Morris maintains that this is not true and that, in fact, Hillary instead was working on reversing the convictions of Black Panthers who had been convicted of murdering police officers.

In the course of doing this she actually went to California to intern with the law firm of Robert Truehaft (who was the former head of the California

85

Communist Party). While there she became acquainted with Saul Alinsky and became a devotee of his.

As has been already noted, Hillary's college thesis was on Saul Alinsky.

Morris notes that shortly after this Hillary was working for the Watergate Committee that was investigating Richard Nixon in Washington, D.C. Unfortunately, Hillary got herself fired from the Committee for stealing documents and then trying to hide them. *Sound familiar?*

As a young lawyer in 1975 one of the few pro bono cases Hillary took on was to defend the accused rapist of a 12 year-old girl. In her defense of the rapist Hillary put this child on trial and accused her of fantasizing about sex with an older man and on and on trying to portray the young victim in this case as the one who provoked the rape. Hillary Rodham won her case, the girl was devastated and a pedophile was put back on the street.

In a 1980 interview where she was asked about the case Hillary quipped and laughed about the fact that she knew the guy was guilty all along, but she got him off anyway.

Audio tapes of Hillary's unseemly, jocular remarks about getting a guilty man off at the expense of a traumatized child have been played on cable news shows and on national radio shows recently, but don't expect to hear about them on any of the biased mainstream networks: you won't. They won't mention this in an effort to cover up for Hillary Clinton just as they have for Barack Obama for the past eight years.

If you are getting your news from ABC, CBS, CNN, NBC, PBS or the New York Times you're not getting news: you're getting propaganda and lies. Yes, I said lies... you're getting the Democratic "Party Line."

As for Hillary Clinton's illustrious career: Hillary was only hired by the prestigious Rose law firm in Little Rock AFTER her husband Bill became the Attorney General in Arkansas and she only made it to partner in that firm AFTER Bill Clinton got elected as governor of the state.

Sounds familiar, doesn't it?

While at this law firm Hillary and Bill got involved in murky and predatory real estate deals with their Whitewater Development Corporation, which was a scam that allegedly took advantage of senior citizens, costing these people their life's savings.

Hillary had to testify before a Grand Jury about this scandal while she was First Lady in the 1990's, but the files that would have proved her degree of involvement in the Whitewater scheme mysteriously disappeared (only to mysteriously reappear two years later) and as a consequence the grand jury probe went nowhere. She, herself, deliberately blocked the FBI from getting to that documentation in the Whitehouse that would have incriminated her. *Once again... sound familiar?*

There also has been a long history of untimely deaths, suicides and murders of people who have associated with or worked for the Clintons. Purportedly these were people who might have posed a risk of letting the truth come out about the Clinton's nefarious and illegal activities.

And this brings us right up to the present as there has recently been a new rash of these untimely deaths, suicides and murders lately, all involving people who were allegedly about to blow the whistle on Hillary and the Democratic Party for various offenses and illegal activities.

As far as Bill and Hillary Clinton go, they had long ago adopted the methods of Joseph Goebbels of Nazi Party fame. One such method is to keep telling a lie often enough that people finally believe it. The Clinton's have employed this technique throughout their careers and still use the technique today.

Joseph Goebbels was Adolf Hitler's Propaganda Minister in the 1930's and 1940's, up to and throughout World War II. He personally fed the news to the German press and they reported it. This too, is how the press operated in the old Soviet Union.

Tragically, this is exactly how our press and media act today in The United States of America. A big step towards totalitarianism...

****

For those who don't believe these scandalous claims about Hillary Clinton's past then turn to her recent history. You'll see many common denominators between her recent endeavors and those of her past.

Hillary says that she's going to reign in the Wall Street "fat cats." But, the facts are that the highest paying donors to her campaign are the fat cats (securities investors) from Wall Street.

And let's not forget that she was getting $250,000 and up for giving half hour speeches to Wall Street groups: totaling millions in her pocket.

Hillary refuses to release the transcripts of those speeches. Wonder why?

It's astounding: her lies never stop. It's gotten so bad now that we have to start asking her what we should believe: the lies that she told us last year; or the lies she's telling us now.

It is truly unbelievable... Hillary knows people think that she is a liar yet she keeps on telling new lies! No matter what you think of this it indicates a real serious problem with either her mental condition or her character.

Also unbelievable is that Democratic voters by and large don't seem to care about Hillary's character, or lack of it. It's not only astounding: it's sad...

In four and a half years as a New York Senator Hillary accomplished almost NOTHING. Her promise to bring 200,000 jobs to the state during her senate campaign netted a whopping 5-6 thousand jobs four years later.

She did, however, work to relax the sanctions on Iran while in the Senate.

But as Secretary of State Hillary Clinton's ineptitude literally threw the world into chaos by allowing and enabling the growth and spread of ISIS and other radical Islamic groups throughout the mid-east and Africa. By the time she was done ISIS had grown to an army of 80,000 fighters with a presence in 22 countries.

Her decisions, along with those of Barack Obama, have armed the ISIS terrorists beyond anything they could have done for themselves, made ISIS a much more formidable enemy and the world a much more dangerous place for everyone.

This may have even been deliberate on Obama's part. But in Hillary's case, it appears to just be that old ineptitude again...

And, Hillary Clinton does not hold the respect of other world leaders at all. Instead she is regarded as a pretender to the throne who can easily be bribed and bought. Ironically, although they are in other countries and not America, these leaders see Hillary Clinton for exactly who she is: an incapable woman who is only in the position she's in because of her husband, which sadly, is true. And this is especially sad since there are so many intelligent women very capable of being president.

A Margaret Thatcher she is not... and everyone knows it.

It is very unlikely that Hillary is going to be able to negotiate anything of import with other world leaders. They know what she's been doing so, not only won't they trust her, but they'll just look at her track record as the U.S. Secretary of State and see how totally inept she is. They certainly know that how untrustworthy she is and that they can't tell her anything that has to be kept confidential. And it is doubtful that they would believe that Hillary would deliver on anything that she promises.

As for her being able to effectively lead the world: given her dismal track record in foreign affairs it is doubtful that any one would follow this woman, either.

In the role of Commander In Chief Hillary will likely NOT have the respect of our military either because of her actions concerning Benghazi. Refusing to provide security after 600 urgent requests and then refusing to send help for U.S. personnel under attack and in danger of being killed for the sake of her political image is a dastardly thing to do. It is wicked beyond measure and it will not be forgiven by our military.

Adding to that sin is the fact that Hillary lied about the incident and its cause to avoid being held culpable for the fiasco. This shows her to be a coward.

And, because of her stance concerning the nation's police Hillary will also not be able to garner the respect of law enforcement at any level. She has betrayed them too. This will, likewise, not be easily forgiven: if at all.

****

In 2011 Hillary said this about the notorious, anti-American billionaire - globalist, George Soros.

"We need people like George Soros, who is willing to step up when it counts."

So just who is George Soros? George Soros is an 85 year-old Hungarian billionaire who emigrated to the west from the Soviet Union communist occupied Hungary.

Ironically, even though he escaped to the western democracies, he hates everything western. He is an open borders advocate and today he is known to provide funding for anti-American, anarchistic groups like Black Lives Matter and the Hispanic radical group, La Raza. He is also known to have funded the destructive hate group Occupy Wall Street.

It should be noted that it has been widely reported that the Democratic Party organized Occupy Wall Street and endorses this group as well as La Raza and Black Lives Matter.

Black Lives Matter and La Raza are both racist groups dedicated to making white Americans submit to their demands. Some of those demands being: reparations to blacks for slavery and the return of the lands in America's southwest to Mexico: including the states New Mexico, Arizona, California and Texas.

The groups mentioned above have all engaged in riots and anarchy directed at bringing about the demise of The United States and George Soros has been a principal financier to them. He also regularly donates large sums to Democratic Party candidates: and especially Hillary Clinton.

To date Soros has donated huge sums ($13,000,000) to Hillary's Super-Pac. So is Hillary beholding to George Soros? *Ask yourself...*

What Hillary Offers

Hillary is running on a platform where she is planning to continue and even expand upon Barack Obama's failed economic and social policies.

She is running with a plan wherein she has stated that she will increase the amount of un-vetted Syrian refugees to be brought here by more than 500%. This will pose unprecedented risks to the American people; especially if she also continues the policies of Barack Obama where surveillance of Mosques is forbidden and Homeland Security is not allowed to know the whereabouts of the refugees once they arrive here.

Hillary Clinton has also stated that she will TOTALLY eliminate the borders of the United States within her first 100 days in office!

This will beckon millions, if not tens of millions, of unskilled immigrants *and their families* into this country and American taxpayers will have to pay for the subsistence (welfare, section 8 housing, education and medical care) of these millions of needy immigrants all for the sake of getting more Democratic voters for "The Party." Hillary Clinton is giving no thought to the Americans who are already here and will have to foot the bill for all of this. It will be many billions of dollars.

Hillary also wants to prohibit fracking (Hydraulic Fracturing) for oil, prohibit domestic oil and natural gas production in the United States and keep America dependent on oil from the mid-east.

Could this be because she took so many millions in contributions to her Clinton Foundation from Saudi Arabia ($25 million alone) and other mid-eastern countries while she was the Secretary of State? *Well, go ahead... Ask yourself...*

Hillary's campaign commercials stipulate that she will put up 500 million solar panels in the U.S. for clean energy.

It has already been convincingly demonstrated that solar technologies are not yet up to the task of meeting our energy needs or replacing the cheap energy currently produced by coal, oil and natural gas in this country: or anywhere else on the planet for that matter.

Hillary has apparently forgotten about Barack Obama's Solyndra fiasco...

She wants to even further cripple the coal industry and put tens of thousands of coal industry employees out of work. This will also dramatically increase energy costs for every individual and every business in The United States.

She says she will create jobs by rebuilding the infrastructure of the country.

Boy, this sounds familiar... Barack Obama promised this same plan in 2008 and he was given $800 billion to use for what he called "shovel ready jobs" to accomplish this. But, not surprisingly, Obama didn't use the money for this. The money went everywhere but to the infrastructure. Virtually nothing has been improved.

Hillary wants to continue Obama Care even though Obama Care is now responsible for doubling and tripling health care costs for the average family and has also considerably lowered the quality of care that is given to patients in this country.

Hillary Clinton's tax strategies will ensure that U.S. companies continue to leave the United States and also keep trillions of dollars of their revenue overseas to avoid the excessive taxation here. At present, The United States has the highest corporate tax rates in the developed world.

Hillary is already reinforcing, and engaging in, Barack Obama's malicious war on the police and his divisive racial policies. She is "piggybacking" on these policies: criticizing the police and giving credibility to the lies being promoted by Barack Obama and Black Lives Matter; once again, all for minority votes. So the damage to the country will continue, the crime will grow and it will spread as will racial strife.

Summing Up Hillary's Plan for America

Hillary offers NO protection against terrorist threats domestically and she has no strategy whatsoever for containing terrorism or defeating it overseas. In fact, rather than contain terrorism while Secretary of State, she expanded it with her foolish policies, which showed alarmingly poor judgment and a complete lack of knowledge of who she was dealing with.

It is frankly shocking that Hillary Clinton couldn't foresee the risks that her policies and plans in the Mid-East posed for the region and the world at large. Her exploitative follies also reveal a startling lack of intelligence.

92

She also offers no plans for protection against potential EMP attacks or Cyber attacks that could cripple our entire country in minutes and send all of us back to the dark ages. Hillary Clinton has yet to even mention these very real threats.

Come to think of it: Hillary may be the wrong person to rely on for cyber security.

In short, Hillary Clinton has absolutely NO new ideas to solve anything and worse yet, she doesn't have the foresight to protect the country from the very real threats that exist for America. The potential EMP and Cyber attacks I've listed actually are existential threats and it's doubtful that she's even aware of them.

Add to that, that Hillary knows absolutely nothing about running a business or businesses of any size. Should she be elected we'll have an economics moron in charge of our country's already weak and stumbling economy. It won't take much to start another severe recession and Hillary's economic plan is literally a recipe for this.

She is offering the very same things that Obama promised in 2008 only in larger amounts: MUCH larger: On steroids.

So the question is: why haven't the Democrats already done these things if they're so good? It's been eight years... they had the money... Why is it that we have to wait now until Hillary is elected?

Ask yourself...

What Hillary does offer are much higher taxes ($1.3 TRILLION in new taxes to start with), bigger deficits ($1.4 TRILLION in higher federal expenditures as *giveaways* to get votes), unproven and expensive energy policies, escalating health insurance costs with lower quality medical care, more federal regulations that stifle new businesses and much higher risks to the U.S. from anti-American factions and countries around the world.

Her decisions and policies in the mid-east were not just bad; they were monumentally bad. Her reset program with Russia also failed miserably and just worsened relations with that country. If she made any points with Russia at all it would have to been for approving the sale of twenty percent of U.S. uranium to Russian owned entities, who are already funneling that resource to their ally Iran for that country's nuclear weapons program.

With regard to foreign affairs decisions and policies, Hillary's incompetence is beyond anything that we have seen from a Secretary of State in 100 years. Her policies and decisions have been nothing short of disastrous. And not only didn't she do anything right: she surreptitiously bent rules and ignored or circumvented laws in the process. Indeed everything she does seems to have her ignoble stamp on it.

Just when will the media's commentators who continually praise her and give her softball interviews report on her real track record?

That's right: Ask yourself why they haven't.

Hillary supporters and the media pundits also are always "lauding" Hillary Clinton's vast foreign policy experience.

What!? Yes, they actually say this and, because of their disdain for average Americans, they expect us all to believe it. If they were talking about a crime family they'd have a point...

Makes one wonder what planet her supporters live on. But, what all of these sycophants deliberately leave out is that Hillary's foreign policies have had universally dismal if not disastrous results. In fact, it's not just her foreign policy endeavors: it's all of her endeavors.

Did I say all...?

Democrats and the media have also tried to brand her as the "smartest woman in the world." They portray her as smart and wise because of her extensive political experience.

Please... Being a deceitful hypocrite who is willing to lie about anything and step on anyone to get ahead doesn't mean a person's smart: it does though, mean they're a charlatan. To that she can lay claim.

As for wise... her direction, policies and activities while Secretary of State do not reflect wisdom: they do, however, reflect a startling lack of it.

They also give the sense of large-scale corruption.

As more and more of the emails from Hillary's time as Secretary of State surface the more clear it is that Hillary Clinton's State Department was as much, if not more, an office set up to rake in millions in "Pay for Play" schemes to enrich the Clintons' foundation from countries and individuals for favors, than it was as an office for the important business of a Secretary of State for the United States. Yes, this is scandalous; especially considering some of the deals that have been approved and arranged by this Secretary of State.

More corruption? As they say: leopards don't change their spots...

Finally, Hillary Clinton's severe risk to our national security just keeps getting worse. It has recently been reported in the book "Infiltration," that Hillary's top aide, closest confidant and the Vice-Chair of her campaign, Huma Abiden, was a journalist for an Islamic magazine that Abiden's mother has published for years and Abedin worked there as a journalist for almost thirteen years. Abedin's mother happens to believe in Sharia law: which endorses wife beatings, marital rape, stoning women to death for adultery, the subservience of women to men in all instances, the persecution and execution of homosexuals, etc.

What does this have to do with national security, you might ask...

Well, it turns out that Hillary personally visited Abedin's mother on a trip to Saudi Arabia: she apparently has a pretty good relationship with this woman. During this visit Huma's mother is said to have asked Hillary to increase the number of visas for Saudis, which Hillary said she would do. And, she in fact, did go ahead and do just that. The number of approved Saudi visas has dramatically increased since this described event. So, why would Hillary Clinton even entertain such a request in the first place?

Ask yourself...

And now literally everyday more information comes out revealing Hillary's nefarious associations and the actions she has taken on behalf of individuals involved in them. It just never seems to end. And, keep in mind that this information is leaking out in spite of a massive cover up that has been going on to keep this information from the American public.

****

We have already suffered through a president who has repeatedly lied to the American people for the last eight years about almost everything: At least everything important. And one who has even betrayed America and put it and its citizens at needless risk.

And we have also had a dishonest press that has not called this president out for his lies and betrayals: and by omitting deserved criticism of him have lied themselves by that omission, thereby betraying their journalistic ethics and responsibility to the public.

America cannot afford this anymore: ANY OF IT!

And America cannot afford or endure another chief executive of Barack Obama's ilk. But that is exactly what Americans will get should Hillary Clinton be elected as our next chief executive.

****

Sources

Online, Radio and Print:

Americannews.com
AP.org (the Associated Press)
Beforeitsnews.com
TheBlaze.com
BostonGlobe.com
Buck Sexton/the Rush Limbaugh program
Foxnews.com
Heather Mac Donald: The War On Cops
Breitbart.com
Conservativetribune.org
The DailyCaller.com
DailyWire.com
Departed Investigativeproject.org
Drudgereport.com
Edward Klein/Ed Klein Confidential
Heritage.org
Ibtimes.com (International Business Times0
Infowars.com
Jewsnews.com
Jihadwatch.org
Judicialwatch.org
LATimes.com
NationalReview.com
NewYorkPost.com
NyTimes.com
The O'Reilly Factor
Proflagnews.com
The Rush Limbaugh Show
The Sean Hannity (radio show)
Teaparty.org
Thepoliticalinsider.org
Truthandaction.org
The Sundowner – wordpress
USApoliticsNow.com

WashingtonExaminer.com
WashingtonTimes.com
Westernjournalism.com
Wikileaks.org/Julian Assange
Wnd.com/WorldNetDaily

TV Networks
ABC News
CBS News
FOX News
NBC News

****

The Constitution of The United States

We the People of the United States, in Order to form a more perfect Union, establish Justice, insure domestic Tranquility, provide for the common defence, promote the general Welfare, and secure the Blessings of Liberty to ourselves and our Posterity, do ordain and establish this Constitution for the United States of America.

Article 1.

Section 1

All legislative Powers herein granted shall be vested in a Congress of the United States, which shall consist of a Senate and House of Representatives.

Section 2

The House of Representatives shall be composed of Members chosen every second Year by the People of the several States, and the Electors in each State shall have the Qualifications requisite for Electors of the most numerous Branch of the State Legislature.

No Person shall be a Representative who shall not have attained to the Age of twenty five Years, and been seven Years a Citizen of the United States, and who shall not, when elected, be an Inhabitant of that State in which he shall be chosen.

Representatives and direct Taxes shall be apportioned among the several States which may be included within this Union, according to their respective Numbers,which shall be determined by adding to the whole Number of free Persons, including those bound to Service for a Term of Years, and excluding Indians not taxed, three fifths of all other Persons.

The actual Enumeration shall be made within three Years after the first Meeting of the Congress of the United States, and within every subsequent Term of ten Years, in such Manner as they shall by Law direct. The Number of Representatives shall not exceed one for every thirty Thousand, but each State shall have at Least one Representative; and until such enumeration shall be made, the State of New Hampshire shall be entitled to choose three, Massachusetts eight, Rhode Island and Providence Plantations one, Connecticut five, New York six, New Jersey four, Pennsylvania eight, Delaware one, Maryland six, Virginia ten, North Carolina five, South Carolina five and Georgia three.When vacancies happen in the Representation from any State, the Executive Authority thereof shall issue Writs of Election to fill such Vacancies.

The House of Representatives shall choose their Speaker and other Officers; and shall have the sole Power of Impeachment.

Section 3

The Senate of the United States shall be composed of two Senators from each State, chosen by the Legislature thereof, for six Years; and each Senator shall have one Vote.

Immediately after they shall be assembled in Consequence of the first Election, they shall be divided as equally as may be into three Classes. The Seats of the Senators of the first Class shall be vacated at the Expiration of the second Year, of the second Class at the Expiration of the fourth Year, and of the third Class at the Expiration of the sixth Year, so that one third may be chosen every second Year; and if Vacancies happen by Resignation, or otherwise, during the Recess of the Legislature of any State, the Executive thereof may make temporary Appointments until the next Meeting of the Legislature, which shall then fill such Vacancies.

No person shall be a Senator who shall not have attained to the Age of thirty Years, and been nine Years a Citizen of the United States, and who shall not, when elected, be an Inhabitant of that State for which he shall be chosen.

The Vice President of the United States shall be President of the Senate, but shall have no Vote, unless they be equally divided.

The Senate shall choose their other Officers, and also a President pro tempore, in the absence of the Vice President, or when he shall exercise the Office of President of the United States.

The Senate shall have the sole Power to try all Impeachments. When sitting for that Purpose, they shall be on Oath or Affirmation. When the President of the United States is tried, the Chief Justice shall preside: And no Person shall be convicted without the Concurrence of two thirds of the Members present.

Judgment in Cases of Impeachment shall not extend further than to removal from Office, and disqualification to hold and enjoy any Office of honor, Trust or Profit under the United States: but the Party convicted shall nevertheless be liable and subject to Indictment, Trial, Judgment and Punishment, according to Law.

Section 4

The Times, Places and Manner of holding Elections for Senators and Representatives, shall be prescribed in each State by the Legislature thereof; but the Congress may at any time by Law make or alter such Regulations, except as to the Place of Choosing Senators.

The Congress shall assemble at least once in every Year, and such Meeting shall be on the first Monday in December, unless they shall by Law appoint a different Day.

Section 5

Each House shall be the Judge of the Elections, Returns and Qualifications of its own Members, and a Majority of each shall constitute a Quorum to do Business; but a smaller number may adjourn from day to day, and may be authorized to compel the Attendance of absent Members, in such Manner, and under such Penalties as each House may provide.

Each House may determine the Rules of its Proceedings, punish its Members for disorderly Behavior, and, with the Concurrence of two-thirds, expel a Member.

Each House shall keep a Journal of its Proceedings, and from time to time publish the same, excepting such Parts as may in their Judgment require Secrecy; and the Yeas and Nays of the Members of either House on any question shall, at the Desire of one fifth of those Present, be entered on the Journal.

Neither House, during the Session of Congress, shall, without the Consent of the other, adjourn for more than three days, nor to any other Place than that in which the two Houses shall be sitting.

Section 6

The Senators and Representatives shall receive a Compensation for their Services, to be ascertained by Law, and paid out of the Treasury of the United States. They shall in all Cases, except Treason, Felony and Breach of the Peace, be privileged from Arrest during their Attendance at the Session of their respective Houses, and in going to and returning from the same; and for any Speech or Debate in either House, they shall not be questioned in any other Place.

No Senator or Representative shall, during the Time for which he was elected, be appointed to any civil Office under the Authority of the United States which shall have been created, or the Emoluments whereof shall have been increased during such time; and no Person holding any Office under the United States, shall be a Member of either House during his Continuance in Office.

Section 7

All bills for raising Revenue shall originate in the House of Representatives; but the Senate may propose or concur with Amendments as on other Bills.

Every Bill which shall have passed the House of Representatives and the Senate, shall, before it become a Law, be presented to the President of the United States; If he approve he shall sign it, but if not he shall return it, with his Objections to that House in which it shall have originated, who shall enter theObjections at large on their Journal, and proceed to reconsider it. If after such Reconsideration two thirds of that House shall agree to pass the Bill, it shall be sent, together with the Objections, to the other House, by which it shall likewise be reconsidered, and if approved by two thirds of that House, it shall become a Law. But in all such Cases the Votes of both Houses shall be determined by Yeas and Nays, and the Names of the Persons voting for and against the Bill shall be entered on the Journal of each House respectively. If any Bill shall not be returned by the President within ten Days (Sundays excepted) after it shall have been presented to him, the Same shall be a Law, in like Manner as if he had signed it, unless the Congress by their Adjournment prevent its Return, in which Case it shall not be a Law.

Every Order, Resolution, or Vote to which the Concurrence of the Senate and House of Representatives may be necessary (except on a question of Adjournment) shall be presented to the President of the United States; and before the Same shall take Effect, shall be approved by him, or being disapproved by him, shall be repassed by two thirds of the Senate and House of Representatives, according to the Rules and Limitations prescribed in the Case of a Bill.

Section 8

The Congress shall have Power To lay and collect Taxes, Duties, Imposts and Excises, to pay the Debts and provide for the common Defence and generalWelfare of the United States; but all Duties, Imposts and Excises shall be uniform throughout the United States; To borrow money on the credit of the United States;

To regulate Commerce with foreign Nations, and among the several States, and with the Indian Tribes; To establish an uniform Rule of Naturalization, and uniform Laws on the subject of Bankruptcies throughout the United States;

To coin Money, regulate the Value thereof, and of foreign Coin, and fix the Standard of Weights and Measures;

To provide for the Punishment of counterfeiting the Securities and current Coin of the United States;

To establish Post Offices and Post Roads;

To promote the Progress of Science and useful Arts, by securing for limited Times to Authors and Inventors the exclusive Right to their respective Writings and Discoveries;

To constitute Tribunals inferior to the supreme Court;

To define and punish Piracies and Felonies committed on the high Seas, and Offenses against the Law of Nations;

To declare War, grant Letters of Marque and Reprisal, and make Rules concerning Captures on Land and Water;

To raise and support Armies, but no Appropriation of Money to that Use shall be for a longer Term than two Years;

To provide and maintain a Navy;

To make Rules for the Government and Regulation of the land and naval Forces;

To provide for calling forth the Militia to execute the Laws of the Union, suppress Insurrections and repel Invasions;

To provide for organizing, arming, and disciplining, the Militia, and for governing such Part of them as may be employed in the Service of the United States, reserving to the States respectively, the Appointment of the Officers, and the Authority of training the Militia according to the discipline prescribed by Congress;

To exercise exclusive Legislation in all Cases whatsoever, over such District (not exceeding ten Miles square) as may, by Cession of particular States, and the acceptance of Congress, become the Seat of the Government of the United States, and to exercise like Authority over all Places purchased by the Consent of the Legislature of the State in which the Same shall be, for the Erection of Forts, Magazines, Arsenals, dock-Yards, and other needful Buildings; And To make all Laws which shall be necessary and proper for carrying into Execution the foregoing Powers, and all other Powers vested by this Constitution in the Government of the United States, or in any Department or Officer thereof.

Section 9

The Migration or Importation of such Persons as any of the States now existing shall think proper to admit, shall not be prohibited by the Congress prior to the Year one thousand eight hundred and eight, but a tax or duty may be imposed on such Importation, not exceeding ten dollars for each Person.

The privilege of the Writ of Habeas Corpus shall not be suspended, unless when in Cases of Rebellion or Invasion the public Safety may require it.

No Bill of Attainder or ex post facto Law shall be passed.

No capitation, or other direct, Tax shall be laid, unless in Proportion to the Census or Enumeration herein before directed to be taken.

No Tax or Duty shall be laid on Articles exported from any State.

No Preference shall be given by any Regulation of Commerce or Revenue to the Ports of one State over those of another: nor shall Vessels bound to, or from, one State, be obliged to enter, clear, or pay Duties in another.

No Money shall be drawn from the Treasury, but in Consequence of Appropriations made by Law; and a regular Statement and Account of the Receipts and
Expenditures of all public Money shall be published from time to time.

No Title of Nobility shall be granted by the United States: And no Person holding any Office of Profit or Trust under them, shall, without the Consent of the Congress, accept of any present, Emolument, Office, or Title, of any kind whatever, from any King, Prince or foreign State.

Section 10

No State shall enter into any Treaty, Alliance, or Confederation; grant Letters of Marque and Reprisal; coin Money; emit Bills of Credit; make any Thing but gold and silver Coin a Tender in Payment of Debts; pass any Bill of Attainder, ex post facto Law, or Law impairing the Obligation of Contracts, or grant any Title of Nobility.

No State shall, without the Consent of the Congress, lay any Imposts or Duties on Imports or Exports, except what may be absolutely necessary for executing its inspection Laws: and the net Produce of all Duties and Imposts, laid by any State on Imports or Exports, shall be for the Use of the Treasury of the United

States; and all such Laws shall be subject to the Revision and Control of the Congress.

No State shall, without the Consent of Congress, lay any duty of Tonnage, keep Troops, or Ships of War in time of Peace, enter into any Agreement or Compact with another State, or with a foreign Power, or engage in War, unless actually invaded, or in such imminent Danger as will not admit of delay.

Article 2.

Section 1

The executive Power shall be vested in a President of the United States of America. He shall hold his Office during the Term of four Years, and, together with the Vice-President chosen for the same Term, be elected, as follows:

Each State shall appoint, in such Manner as the Legislature thereof may direct, a Number of Electors, equal to the whole Number of Senators and Representatives to which the State may be entitled in the Congress: but no Senator or Representative, or Person holding an Office of Trust or Profit under the United States, shall be appointed an Elector.

The Electors shall meet in their respective States, and vote by Ballot for two persons, of whom one at least shall not lie an Inhabitant of the same State with themselves. And they shall make a List of all the Persons voted for, and of the Number of Votes for each; which List they shall sign and certify, and transmit sealed to the Seat of the Government of the United States, directed to the President of the Senate. The President of the Senate shall, in the Presence of the Senate and House of Representatives, open all the Certificates, and the Votes shall then be counted. The Person having the greatest Number of Votes shall be the President, if such Number be a Majority of the whole Number of Electors appointed; and if there be more than one who have such Majority, and have an equal Number of Votes, then the House of Representatives shall immediately choose by Ballot one of them for President; and if no Person have aMajority, then from the five highest on the List the said House shall in like Manner choose the President. But in choosing the President, the Votes shall be taken by States, the Representation from each State having one Vote; a quorum for this Purpose shall consist of a Member or Members from two-thirds of the States, and a Majority of all the States shall be necessary to a

Choice. In every Case, after the Choice of the President, the Person having the greatest Number of Votes of the Electors shall be the Vice President. But if there should remain two or more who have equal Votes, the Senate shall choose from them by Ballot the Vice-President.

The Congress may determine the Time of choosing the Electors, and the Day on which they shall give their Votes; which Day shall be the same throughout the United States.

No person except a natural born Citizen, or a Citizen of the United States, at the time of the Adoption of this Constitution, shall be eligible to the Office of President; neither shall any Person be eligible to that Office who shall not have attained to the Age of thirty-five Years, and been fourteen Years a Resident within the United States.

In Case of the Removal of the President from Office, or of his Death, Resignation, or Inability to discharge the Powers and Duties of the said Office, the same shall devolve on the Vice President, and the Congress may by Law provide for the Case of Removal, Death, Resignation or Inability, both of the President and Vice President, declaring what Officer shall then act as President, and such Officer shall act accordingly, until the Disability be removed, or a President shall be elected.

The President shall, at stated Times, receive for his Services, a Compensation, which shall neither be increased nor diminished during the Period for which he shall have been elected, and he shall not receive within that Period any other Emolument from the United States, or any of them.

Before he enter on the Execution of his Office, he shall take the following Oath or Affirmation:

"I do solemnly swear (or affirm) that I will faithfully execute the Office of President of the United States, and will to the best of my Ability, preserve, protect and defend the Constitution of the United States."

Section 2

The President shall be Commander in Chief of the Army and Navy of the United States, and of the Militia of the several States, when called into the actual

Service of the United States; he may require the Opinion, in writing, of the principal Officer in each of the executive Departments, upon any subject relating to the Duties of their respective Offices, and he shall have Power to Grant Reprieves and Pardons for Offenses against the United States, except in Cases of Impeachment.

He shall have Power, by and with the Advice and Consent of the Senate, to make Treaties, provided two thirds of the Senators present concur; and he shall nominate, and by and with the Advice and Consent of the Senate, shall appoint Ambassadors, other public Ministers and Consuls, Judges of the supreme Court, and all other Officers of the United States, whose Appointments are not herein otherwise provided for, and which shall be established by Law: but the Congress may by Law vest the Appointment of such inferior Officers, as they think proper, in the President alone, in the Courts of Law, or in the Heads of Departments.

The President shall have Power to fill up all Vacancies that may happen during the Recess of the Senate, by granting Commissions which shall expire at the End of their next Session.

Section 3

He shall from time to time give to the Congress Information of the State of the Union, and recommend to their Consideration such Measures as he shall judge necessary and expedient; he may, on extraordinary Occasions, convene both Houses, or either of them, and in Case of Disagreement between them, with Respect to the Time of Adjournment, he may adjourn them to such Time as he shall think proper; he shall receive Ambassadors and other public Ministers; he shall take Care that the Laws be faithfully executed, and shall Commission all the Officers of the United States.

Section 4

The President, Vice President and all civil Officers of the United States, shall be removed from Office on Impeachment for, and Conviction of, Treason, Bribery, or other high Crimes and Misdemeanors.

Article 3.

Section 1

The judicial Power of the United States, shall be vested in one supreme Court, and in such inferior Courts as the Congress may from time to time ordain and establish. The Judges, both of the supreme and inferior Courts, shall hold their Offices during good Behavior, and shall, at stated Times, receive for their Services a Compensation which shall not be diminished during their Continuance in Office.

Section 2

The judicial Power shall extend to all Cases, in Law and Equity, arising under this Constitution, the Laws of the United States, and Treaties made, or which shall be made, under their Authority; to all Cases affecting Ambassadors, other public Ministers and Consuls; to all Cases of admiralty and maritimeJurisdiction; to Controversies to which the United States shall be a Party; to Controversies between two or more States; between a State and Citizens of another State; between Citizens of different States; between Citizens of the same State claiming Lands under Grants of different States, and between a State, or the Citizens thereof, and foreign States, Citizens or Subjects.

In all Cases affecting Ambassadors, other public Ministers and Consuls, and those in which a State shall be Party, the supreme Court shall have originalJurisdiction. In all the other Cases before mentioned, the supreme Court shall have appellate Jurisdiction, both as to Law and Fact, with such Exceptions, and under such Regulations as the Congress shall make.

The Trial of all Crimes, except in Cases of Impeachment, shall be by Jury; and such Trial shall be held in the State where the said Crimes shall have been committed; but when not committed within any State, the Trial shall be at such Place or Places as the Congress may by Law have directed.

Section 3

Treason against the United States, shall consist only in levying War against them, or in adhering to their Enemies, giving them Aid and Comfort. No Person shall be convicted of Treason unless on the Testimony of two Witnesses to the same overt Act, or on Confession in open Court.

The Congress shall have power to declare the Punishment of Treason, but no Attainder of Treason shall work Corruption of Blood, or Forfeiture except during the Life of the Person attainted.

Article 4.

Section 1

Full Faith and Credit shall be given in each State to the public Acts, Records, and judicial Proceedings of every other State. And the Congress may by general Laws prescribe the Manner in which such Acts, Records and Proceedings shall be proved, and the Effect thereof.

Section 2

The Citizens of each State shall be entitled to all Privileges and Immunities of Citizens in the several States.

A Person charged in any State with Treason, Felony, or other Crime, who shall flee from Justice, and be found in another State, shall on demand of the executive Authority of the State from which he fled, be delivered up, to be removed to the State having Jurisdiction of the Crime.

No Person held to Service or Labour in one State, under the Laws thereof, escaping into another, shall, in Consequence of any Law or Regulation therein, be discharged from such Service or Labour, But shall be delivered up on Claim of the Party to whom such Service or Labour may be due.

Section 3

New States may be admitted by the Congress into this Union; but no new States shall be formed or erected within the Jurisdiction of any other State; nor any State be formed by the Junction of two or more States, or parts of States, without the Consent of the Legislatures of the States concerned as well as of the Congress.

The Congress shall have Power to dispose of and make all needful Rules and Regulations respecting the Territory or other Property belonging to the United States; and nothing in this Constitution shall be so construed as to Prejudice any Claims of the United States, or of any particular State.

Section 4

The United States shall guarantee to every State in this Union a Republican Form of Government, and shall protect each of them against Invasion; and onApplication of the Legislature, or of the Executive (when the Legislature cannot be convened) against domestic Violence.

Article 5

The Congress, whenever two thirds of both Houses shall deem it necessary, shall propose Amendments to this Constitution, or, on the Application of the Legislatures of two thirds of the several States, shall call a Convention for proposing Amendments, which, in either Case, shall be valid to all Intents and Purposes, as part of this Constitution, when ratified by the Legislatures of three fourths of the several States, or by Conventions in three fourths thereof, as the one or the other Mode of Ratification may be proposed by the Congress; Provided that no Amendment which may be made prior to the Year One thousand eight hundred and eight shall in any Manner affect the first and fourth Clauses in the Ninth Section of the first Article; and that no State, without its Consent, shall be deprived of its equal Suffrage in the Senate.

Article 6

All Debts contracted and Engagements entered into, before the Adoption of this Constitution, shall be as valid against the United States under this Constitution, as under the Confederation.

This Constitution, and the Laws of the United States which shall be made in Pursuance thereof; and all Treaties made, or which shall be made, under theAuthority of the United States, shall be the supreme Law of the Land; and the Judges in every State shall be bound thereby, any Thing in the Constitution orLaws of any State to the Contrary notwithstanding.

The Senators and Representatives before mentioned, and the Members of the several State Legislatures, and all executive and judicial Officers, both of the United States and of the several States, shall be bound by Oath or Affirmation, to support this Constitution; but no religious Test shall ever be required as a Qualification to any Office or public Trust under the United States.

Article 7.

The Ratification of the Conventions of nine States, shall be sufficient for the Establishment of this Constitution between the States so ratifying the Same.

Done in Convention by the Unanimous Consent of the States present the Seventeenth Day of September in the Year of our Lord one thousand seven hundred and Eighty seven and of the Independence of the United States of America the Twelfth. In Witness whereof We have hereunto subscribed our Names.

George Washington - President and deputy from Virginia

New Hampshire - John Langdon, Nicholas Gilman

Massachusetts - Nathaniel Gorham, Rufus King

Connecticut - William Samuel Johnson, Roger Sherman

New York - Alexander Hamilton

New Jersey - William Livingston, David Brearley, William Paterson, Jonathan Dayton

Pennsylvania - Benjamin Franklin, Thomas Mifflin, Robert Morris, George Clymer, Thomas Fitzsimons, Jared Ingersoll, James Wilson, Gouvernour Morris

Delaware - George Read, Gunning Bedford Jr., John Dickinson, Richard Bassett, Jacob Broom

Maryland - James McHenry, Daniel of St Thomas Jenifer, Daniel Carroll

Virginia - John Blair, James Madison Jr.

North Carolina - William Blount, Richard Dobbs Spaight, Hugh Williamson

South Carolina - John Rutledge, Charles Cotesworth Pinckney, Charles Pinckney, Pierce Butler

Georgia - William Few, Abraham Baldwin

Attest: William Jackson, Secretary

Amendment 1

Congress shall make no law respecting an establishment of religion, or prohibiting the free exercise thereof; or abridging the freedom of speech, or of the press; or the right of the people peaceably to assemble, and to petition the Government for a redress of grievances.

Amendment 2

A well regulated Militia, being necessary to the security of a free State, the right of the people to keep and bear Arms, shall not be infringed.

Amendment 3

No Soldier shall, in time of peace be quartered in any house, without the consent of the Owner, nor in time of war, but in a manner to be prescribed by law.

Amendment 4

The right of the people to be secure in their persons, houses, papers, and effects, against unreasonable searches and seizures, shall not be violated, and no Warrants shall issue, but upon probable cause, supported by Oath or affirmation, and particularly describing the place to be searched, and the persons or things to be seized.

Amendment 5

No person shall be held to answer for a capital, or otherwise infamous crime, unless on a presentment or indictment of a Grand Jury, except in cases arising in the land or naval forces, or in the Militia, when in actual service in time of War or public danger; nor shall any person be subject for the same offense to be twice put in jeopardy of life or limb; nor shall be compelled in any criminal case to be a witness against himself, nor be deprived of life, liberty, or property, without due process of law; nor shall private property be taken for public use, without just compensation.

Amendment 6

In all criminal prosecutions, the accused shall enjoy the right to a speedy and public trial, by an impartial jury of the State and district wherein the crime shall have been committed, which district shall have been previously ascertained by law, and to be informed of the nature and cause of the accusation; to be confronted with the witnesses against him; to have compulsory process for obtaining witnesses in his favor, and to have the Assistance of Counsel for his defence.

Amendment 7

In Suits at common law, where the value in controversy shall exceed twenty dollars, the right of trial by jury shall be preserved, and no fact tried by a jury, shall be otherwise re-examined in any Court of the United States, than according to the rules of the common law.

Amendment 8

Excessive bail shall not be required, nor excessive fines imposed, nor cruel and unusual punishments inflicted.

Amendment 9

The enumeration in the Constitution, of certain rights, shall not be construed to deny or disparage others retained by the people.

Amendment 10

The powers not delegated to the United States by the Constitution, nor prohibited by it to the States, are reserved to the States respectively, or to the people.

Amendment 11

The Judicial power of the United States shall not be construed to extend to any suit in law or equity, commenced or prosecuted against one of the United States by Citizens of another State, or by Citizens or Subjects of any Foreign State.

Amendment 12

The Electors shall meet in their respective states, and vote by ballot for President and Vice-President, one of whom, at least, shall not be an inhabitant of the same state with themselves; they shall name in their ballots the person voted for as President, and in distinct ballots the person voted for as Vice-President, and they shall make distinct lists of all persons voted for as President, and of all persons voted for as Vice-President and of the number of votes for each, which lists they shall sign and certify, and transmit sealed to the seat of the government of the United States, directed to the President of the Senate;

The President of the Senate shall, in the presence of the Senate and House of Representatives, open all the certificates and the votes shall then be counted;

The person having the greatest Number of votes for President, shall be the President, if such number be a majority of the whole number of Electors appointed; and if no person have such majority, then from the persons having the highest numbers not exceeding three on the list of those voted for as President, the House of Representatives shall choose immediately, by ballot, the President. But in choosing the President, the votes shall be taken by states, the representation from each state having one vote; a quorum for this purpose shall consist of a member or members from two-thirds of the states, and a majority of all the states shall be necessary to a choice. And if the House of Representatives shall not choose a President whenever the right of choice shall devolve upon them, before the fourth day of March next following, then the Vice-President shall act as President, as in the case of the death or other constitutional disability of the President.

The person having the greatest number of votes as Vice-President, shall be the Vice-President, if such number be a majority of the whole number of Electors appointed, and if no person have a majority, then from the two highest numbers on the list, the Senate shall choose the Vice-President; a quorum for the purpose shall consist of two-thirds of the whole number of Senators, and a majority of the whole number shall be necessary to a choice. But no person constitutionally ineligible to the office of President shall be eligible to that of Vice-President of the United States.

Amendment 13

1. Neither slavery nor involuntary servitude, except as a punishment for crime whereof the party shall have been duly convicted, shall exist within the United States, or any place subject to their jurisdiction.

2. Congress shall have power to enforce this article by appropriate legislation.

Amendment 14

1. All persons born or naturalized in the United States, and subject to the jurisdiction thereof, are citizens of the United States and of the State wherein they reside. No State shall make or enforce any law which shall abridge the privileges or immunities of citizens of the United States; nor shall any State deprive any person of life, liberty, or property, without due process of law; nor deny to any person within its jurisdiction the equal protection of the laws.

2. Representatives shall be apportioned among the several States according to their respective numbers, counting the whole number of persons in each State, excluding Indians not taxed. But when the right to vote at any election for the choice of electors for President and Vice-President of the United States, Representatives in Congress, the Executive and Judicial officers of a State, or the members of the Legislature thereof, is denied to any of the male inhabitants of such State, being twenty-one years of age, and citizens of the United States, or in any way abridged, except for participation in rebellion, or other crime, the basis of representation therein shall be reduced in the proportion which the number of such male citizens shall bear to the whole number of male citizens twenty-one years of age in such State.

3. No person shall be a Senator or Representative in Congress, or elector of President and Vice-President, or hold any office, civil or military, under the United States, or under any State, who, having previously taken an oath, as a member of Congress, or as an officer of the United States, or as a member of any State legislature, or as an executive or judicial officer of any State, to support the Constitution of the United States, shall have engaged in insurrection or rebellion against the same, or given aid or comfort to the

enemies thereof. But Congress may by a vote of two-thirds of each House, remove such disability.

4. The validity of the public debt of the United States, authorized by law, including debts incurred for payment of pensions and bounties for services in suppressing insurrection or rebellion, shall not be questioned. But neither the United States nor any State shall assume or pay any debt or obligation incurred in aid of insurrection or rebellion against the United States, or any claim for the loss or emancipation of any slave; but all such debts, obligations and claims shall be held illegal and void.

5. The Congress shall have power to enforce, by appropriate legislation, the provisions of this article.

Amendment 15

1. The right of citizens of the United States to vote shall not be denied or abridged by the United States or by any State on account of race, color, or previous condition of servitude.

2. The Congress shall have power to enforce this article by appropriate legislation.

Amendment 16

The Congress shall have power to lay and collect taxes on incomes, from whatever source derived, without apportionment among the several States, and without regard to any census or enumeration.

Amendment 17

The Senate of the United States shall be composed of two Senators from each State, elected by the people thereof, for six years; and each Senator shall have one vote. The electors in each State shall have the qualifications requisite for electors of the most numerous branch of the State legislatures.

When vacancies happen in the representation of any State in the Senate, the executive authority of such State shall issue writs of election to fill such vacancies: Provided, That the legislature of any State may empower the executive thereof to make temporary appointments until the people fill the vacancies by election as the legislature may direct.

This amendment shall not be so construed as to affect the election or term of any Senator chosen before it becomes valid as part of the Constitution.

Amendment 18

1. After one year from the ratification of this article the manufacture, sale, or transportation of intoxicating liquors within, the importation thereof into, or the exportation thereof from the United States and all territory subject to the jurisdiction thereof for beverage purposes is hereby prohibited.

2. The Congress and the several States shall have concurrent power to enforce this article by appropriate legislation.

3. This article shall be inoperative unless it shall have been ratified as an amendment to the Constitution by the legislatures of the several States, as provided in the Constitution, within seven years from the date of the submission hereof to the States by the Congress.

Amendment 19

The right of citizens of the United States to vote shall not be denied or abridged by the United States or by any State on account of sex.

Congress shall have power to enforce this article by appropriate legislation.

Amendment 20

1. The terms of the President and Vice President shall end at noon on the 20th day of January, and the terms of Senators and Representatives at noon on the 3d day of January, of the years in which such terms would have ended if this article had not been ratified; and the terms of their successors shall then begin.

2. The Congress shall assemble at least once in every year, and such meeting shall begin at noon on the 3d day of January, unless they shall by law appoint a different day.

3. If, at the time fixed for the beginning of the term of the President, the President elect shall have died, the Vice President elect shall become President. If a President shall not have been chosen before the time fixed for the beginning of his term, or if the President elect shall have failed to qualify, then the Vice President elect shall act as President until a President shall have qualified; and the Congress may by law provide for the case wherein neither a President elect nor a Vice President elect shall have qualified, declaring who shall then act as President, or the manner in which one who is to act shall be selected, and such person shall act accordingly until a President or Vice President shall have qualified.

4. The Congress may by law provide for the case of the death of any of the persons from whom the House of Representatives may choose a President whenever the right of choice shall have devolved upon them, and for the case of the death of any of the persons from whom the Senate may choose a Vice President whenever the right of choice shall have devolved upon them.

5. Sections 1 and 2 shall take effect on the 15th day of October following the ratification of this article.

6. This article shall be inoperative unless it shall have been ratified as an amendment to the Constitution by the legislatures of three-fourths of the several States within seven years from the date of its submission.

Amendment 21

1. The eighteenth article of amendment to the Constitution of the United States is hereby repealed.

2. The transportation or importation into any State, Territory, or possession of the United States for delivery or use therein of intoxicating liquors, inviolation of the laws thereof, is hereby prohibited.

3. The article shall be inoperative unless it shall have been ratified as an amendment to the Constitution by conventions in the several States, as provided in the Constitution, within seven years from the date of the submission hereof to the States by the Congress.

Amendment 22

1. No person shall be elected to the office of the President more than twice, and no person who has held the office of President, or acted as President, for more than two years of a term to which some other person was elected President shall be elected to the office of the President more than once. But this Article shall not apply to any person holding the office of President, when this Article was proposed by the Congress, and shall not prevent any person who may be holding the office of President, or acting as President, during the term within which this Article becomes operative from holding the office of President or acting as President during the remainder of such term.

2. This article shall be inoperative unless it shall have been ratified as an amendment to the Constitution by the legislatures of three-fourths of the several States within seven years from the date of its submission to the States by the Congress.

Amendment 23

1. The District constituting the seat of Government of the United States shall appoint in such manner as the Congress may direct: A number of electors of President and Vice President equal to the whole number of Senators and Representatives in Congress to which the District would be entitled if it were a State, but in no event more than the least populous State; they shall be in addition to those appointed by the States, but they shall be considered, for the purposes of the election of President and Vice President, to be electors appointed by a State; and they shall meet in the District and perform such duties as provided by the twelfth article of amendment.

2. The Congress shall have power to enforce this article by appropriate legislation.

Amendment 24

1. The right of citizens of the United States to vote in any primary or other election for President or Vice President, for electors for President or Vice President, or for Senator or Representative in Congress, shall not be denied or abridged by the United States or any State by reason of failure to pay any poll tax or other tax.

2. The Congress shall have power to enforce this article by appropriate legislation.

Amendment 25

1. In case of the removal of the President from office or of his death or resignation, the Vice President shall become President.

2. Whenever there is a vacancy in the office of the Vice President, the President shall nominate a Vice President who shall take office upon confirmation by a majority vote of both Houses of Congress.

3. Whenever the President transmits to the President pro tempore of the Senate and the Speaker of the House of Representatives his written declaration that he is unable to discharge the powers and duties of his office, and until he transmits to them a written declaration to the contrary, such powers and duties shall be discharged by the Vice President as Acting President.

4. Whenever the Vice President and a majority of either the principal officers of the executive departments or of such other body as Congress may by law provide, transmit to the President pro tempore of the Senate and the Speaker of the House of Representatives their written declaration that the President is unable to discharge the powers and duties of his office, the Vice President shall immediately assume the powers and duties of the office as Acting President.

Thereafter, when the President transmits to the President pro tempore of the Senate and the Speaker of the House of Representatives his written declaration that no inability exists, he shall resume the powers and duties of his office unless the Vice President and a majority of either the principal officers of the executive department or of such other body as Congress may by law provide, transmit within four days to the President pro tempore of the Senate and the Speaker of the House of Representatives their written declaration that the President is unable to discharge the powers and duties of his office. Thereupon Congress shall decide the issue, assembling within forty eight hours for that purpose if not in session. If the Congress, within twenty one days after receipt of the latter written declaration, or, if Congress is not in session, within twenty one days after Congress is required to assemble, determines by two thirds vote of both Houses that the President is unable to discharge the powers and duties of his office, the Vice President shall continue to discharge the same as Acting President; otherwise, the President shall resume the powers and duties of his office.

Amendment 26

1. The right of citizens of the United States, who are eighteen years of age or older, to vote shall not be denied or abridged by the United States or by any State on account of age.

2. The Congress shall have power to enforce this article by appropriate legislation.

Amendment 27

No law, varying the compensation for the services of the Senators and Representatives, shall take effect, until an election of Representatives shall have intervened.

The Constitution of The United States was passed and signed on September 17th of 1787